BANG BANG BANG

by Stella Feehily

First performance: 5 September 2011 at Octagon Theatre Bolton

out of joint

Out of Joint is a national and international touring theatre company, developing and producing plays that broaden horizons and investigate our times.

Under the direction of Max Stafford-Clark the company has premiered plays from leading writers including David Hare, Caryl Churchill, David Edgar, Alistair Beaton, Sebastian Barry and Timberlake Wertenbaker, as well as introducing first-time writers such as Stella Feehily and Mark Ravenhill.

Out of Joint co-produces with major theatres across the UK and further afield. Back home, the company pursues an extensive education programme.

"Inventive, individual and humane"
Whatsonstage.com

Keep in touch with Out of Joint
Mailing List: sign up at www.outofjoint.co.uk

Director: **Max Stafford-Clark**
Producer: **Graham Cowley**
Marketing Manager: **Jon Bradfield**
Deputy Producer: **Chantelle Staynings**
Office & Education Administrator: **Panda Cox**
Literary Manager: **Sam Potter**
Finance Officer: **Sandra Rapley**
Associate Director: **Des Kennedy**

Board of Directors Kate Ashfield, Linda Bassett, John Blackmore (Chair), Elyse Dodgson, Sonia Friedman, Stephen Jeffreys, Paul Jesson, Danny Sapani, Karl Sydow

Out of Joint
7 Thane Works, Thane Villas, London N7 7NU
020 7609 0207
ojo@outofjoint.co.uk
www.outofjoint.co.uk

BOOKSHOP:
Buy scripts like this one at discounted rates: www.outofjoint.co.uk

EDUCATION
We offer workshops, resource packs and more. To find out more and get involved, contact Panda at Out of Joint: panda@outofjoint.co.uk / 020 7609 0207.

Out of Joint is grateful to the following for their support over the years: Arts Council England, The Foundation for Sport and the Arts, The Granada Foundation, Yorkshire Bank Charitable Trust, The Baring Foundation, The Paul Hamlyn Foundation, The Olivier Foundation, The Peggy Ramsay Foundation, The John S Cohen Foundation, The David Cohen Charitable Trust, The National Lottery through the Arts Council of England, The Prudential Awards, Stephen Evans, Karl Sydow, Harold Stokes and Friends of Theatre, John Lewis Partnership, Unity Theatre Trust, Royal Victoria Hall Foundation, Harold Hyam Wingate Foundation. Out of Joint is a Registered Charity No. 1033059

octagon
Bolton

Photo © Joel Pammenter

"The most revitalised regional theatre in the country"
The Guardian

The **Octagon Theatre Bolton** is one of the North West's most successful and engaging theatres and has been producing nationally renowned work for more than forty years.

Alongside classic plays, the Octagon has a fine pedigree for presenting new writing by playwrights such as Jim Cartwright, Alan Plater and Tanika Gupta. And the groundbreaking, intimate, flexible auditorium means the plays can take place on thrust or end-on stages, as well as in the round.

The Octagon's activ8 team produce an all-year-round programme of participation and education projects, as well as establishing twelve youth theatre groups at the Octagon and an additional three satellite youth theatre groups across Bolton. Arts Council England referred to activ8's work as "a benchmark for the region".

Bang Bang Bang continues the Octagon's longstanding partnership with Out of Joint, and follows on from the critically acclaimed co-production of *Mixed Up North* in 2009.

Visit www.octagonbolton.co.uk to find out more.

Executive Director: John Blackmore — Artistic Director: David Thacker

Octagon Theatre
Howell Croft South, Bolton
BL1 1SB
Ticket Office: 01204 520661
General Enquiries: 01204 529407
www.octagonbolton.co.uk

Registered Charity Number 248833

Curve is one of Britain's most distinctive, exciting and technologically advanced theatres. Its vision is to delight and challenge audiences of all ages with creative experiences, and involve as many people as possible in enjoying and participating in theatre. Curve are proud supporters of new and emerging talent and actively participate in the development of the next generation of artists, writers and directors. As well as presenting some of the world's finest touring work, Curve produces a varied programme of diverse, exciting and inspiring theatre. Since opening in November 2008, highlights have included the European premiere of *The Light in the Piazza*, Martin McDonagh's *The Pillowman* and, more recently, critically acclaimed revivals of two of Brian Friel's greatest plays, *Molly Sweeney* and *Translations*, and Rodgers and Hammerstein's *The King and I* starring Janie Dee. Previous co-production partners include Headlong, New Perspectives, Akram Khan Company, with the world premieres of *Vertical Road* and *In-I* and Kneehigh, with *The Umbrellas of Cherbourg*. Curve is excited to be co-producing *Bang Bang Bang* as part of its Autumn 2011 season, which includes Curve productions of *One Flew Over the Cuckoo's Nest*, *Buried Child* by Sam Shepard and *42nd Street*.

Curve
Cultural Quarter
Rutland Street
Leicester
LE1 1SB

General enquries: 0116 242 3560 | Ticket office: 0116 242 3595
enquiries@curvetheatre.co.uk | www.curveonline.co.uk

Registered Charity Number 230708

The Royal Court Theatre is Britain's leading national company dedicated to new work by innovative writers from the UK and around the world.

'the most important theatre in Europe' New York Times

ROYAL COURT

autumn 2011

Until 1 Oct

the faith machine
by Alexi Kaye Campbell

2 Dec – 14 Jan

haunted child
by Joe Penhall

13 Oct – 19 Nov

jumpy
by April De Angelis

**In the West End
Apollo Theatre**

From 8 Oct

jerusalem
by Jez Butterworth

'It's hard not to rave about the Royal Court'
Guardian

The Royal Court Theatre for *Bang Bang Bang* on UK Tour

Artistic Director **Dominic Cooke**	Literary Manager **Chris Campbell**	Head of Finance **Helen Perryer**
Executive Director **Kate Horton**	Casting Director **Amy Ball**	Head of Development **Gaby Styles**
General Manager **Catherine Thornborrow**	Head of Production **Paul Handley**	Production Manager **Tariq Rifaat**

Principal sponsor **Coutts**

020 7565 5000
www.royalcourttheatre.com

Sloane Square, London, SW1W 8AS

Supported by
ARTS COUNCIL ENGLAND

SalisburyPlayhouse

Salisbury Playhouse is one of Britain's leading producing theatres, with a national reputation for home-grown work of the highest quality that attracts audiences from across the South West and beyond. It was recently described by the *Daily Telegraph* as "a regional theatre with all guns blazing".

The building comprises the 517-seat Main House, 149-seat Salberg Studio, purpose-built Rehearsal Room and Tesco Community & Education Space. There is also an on-site scenery workshop, wardrobe and props store.

Highlights of 2010/2011 include *The Picture* by Philip Massinger ("dazzlingly revived" *Guardian*), the stage premiere of Michael Morpurgo's *Toro! Toro!* (TMA Award nomination for Best Children's Show) and the musical *Guys and Dolls* (co-produced with Theatr Clwyd Cymru and New Wolsey, Ipswich).

The Playhouse's extensive Participation programme sees more than 14,000 people of all ages engaging with nearly 400 events each year, and the Playhouse's youth theatre, Stage '65, recently celebrated its 45th anniversary.

As well as this production of *Bang Bang Bang*, autumn 2011 at Salisbury Playhouse includes Alan Ayckbourn's *Way Upstream* (complete with water tank and real boat), a new adaptation of Jane Austen's *Persuasion* by Tim Luscombe, and Craig Higginson's *The Girl in the Yellow Dress*.

Salisbury Playhouse gratefully receives funding from **Arts Council England** and **Wiltshire Council**.

The Playhouse is also grateful to **Frank and Elizabeth Brenan** for sponsoring the Salisbury performances of *Bang Bang Bang*.

Artistic Director **Gareth Machin**
Executive Director **Michelle Carwardine-Palmer**

Salisbury Playhouse
Malthouse Lane
Salisbury
Wiltshire
SP2 7RA

General enquiries: 01722 320117 | Ticket office: 01722 320333
info@salisburyplayhouse.com | www.salisburyplayhouse.com

Registered Charity Number 249169

UK TOUR 2011

5–17 September
Octagon Theatre Bolton
01204 520 661
www.octagonbolton.co.uk

21–24 September
North Wall Arts Centre, Oxford
01865 319 450
www.thenorthwall.com

27 September –1 October
Nuffield Theatre, Southampton
023 8067 1771
www.nuffieldtheatre.co.uk

4–8 October
Curve Theatre, Leicester
0116 242 3595
www.curveonline.co.uk

11 October–5 November
Royal Court Theatre, London
020 7565 5000
www.royalcourttheatre.com

9–12 November
Northcott Theatre, Exeter
01392 493493
www.exeternorthcott.co.uk

15–26 November
Salisbury Playhouse
01722 320 333
www.salisburyplayhouse.com

THE COMPANY

Sadhbh	**Orla Fitzgerald**
Mathilde	**Julie Dray**
Soldier/ Colonel Mburame/Innocent	**Babou Ceesay**
Stephen	**Dan Fredenburgh**
Bibi/Woman with sick baby/ Mama Carolina/Female Soldier	**Frances Ashman**
Child Soldier/Amala/ Screaming Child	**Zara Brown** **Pena liyambo** **Akleia Louis-Frederick** **Jessica Richardson**
Ronan/Michael	**Paul Hickey**
Vin	**Jack Farthing**
Director	**Max Stafford-Clark**
Designer	**Miriam Nabarro**
Lighting Designer	**Johanna Town**
Sound Designer	**Andy Smith**
Movement Director	**Mark Murphy**
Associate Director	**Des Kennedy**
Assistant Director	**Kamau Wa Ndung'u**
Costume Supervisor	**Mary Horan**
Dialect Coach	**Penny Dyer**
Company Stage Manager	**Richard Llewelyn**
Stage Manager (Octagon)	**Helen Keast**
Deputy Stage Manager	**Helen Bowen**
Assistant Stage Manager	**Lyndsey Holmes**
Assistant Stage Manager (Octagon)	**Danielle Fearnley**
Production Manager	**Olly Seviour**
Production Manager (tour)	**Matt Noddings**
Set built by	**Octagon Theatre Bolton**
Head of Workshop	**Pete Rimmer**
Workshop Assistants	**Helen Hall, Harry Hearne**
Scenic Painters	**Imogen Peers, Ged Mayo**
Additional Construction	**Steve Bunn**

Miriam Nabarro is grateful for the help of Gwynneth Binyon, Zoe Marriage, Emma Pile, Erik Rehl and Claudia Seymour

BIOGRAPHIES

FRANCES ASHMAN
Bibi/Mother/Mama
Carolina/Female Soldier

Trained Guildhall School of Music & Drama.

Theatre includes: *Duchess of Malfi* (Northampton); *After the Accident* (Soho); *In the Blood* (Finborough); *Pornography* (Birmingham Rep); *Cockroach* (National Theatre of Scotland); *Macbeth, Pericles, The Winter's Tale, Macbett* (Royal Shakespeare Company).

Television includes: *The Reckoning, Doctor Who, Law & Order: UK, Missing, Trial & Retribution, Gunrush, The Bill.*

Film includes: *Maybe One Day, Infidel, Nil by Mouth*; as well as appearing in the film she also wrote and performed 'Peculiar Groove' and 'Pandora' featured on the soundtrack.

ZARA BROWN
Child Soldier/Amala/
Screaming Child

Zara lives in South London with her parents. She attends Newstead Wood School and her favourite subjects are maths, science and ICT. She is learning the piano and her hobbies include athletics, bike riding and dancing.

Zara attends classes in dance, drama and singing at D&B Theatre School in Bromley, Kent. Credits include *The Bill* (ITV); *What's Your News* (Nickelodeon) and a commercial for CBBC. Zara is thrilled to be appearing in *Bang Bang Bang.*

BABOU CEESAY
Soldier/Warlord/
Innocent

Theatre includes: for Out of Joint: *Macbeth* and *The Overwhelming* (with the National Theatre); *Pocket Dream* (Propeller Theatre Company); *Elektra* (Young Vic); *The Gods Weep* (Royal Shakespeare Company); *Doctor Faustus* (Present Moment); *A Midsummer Night's Dream, Merchant of Venice* (Propeller Theatre Company/Watermill); *The Long Goodbye* (The Cockpit Theatre); *Twelfth Night* (Pegasus Theatre); *Suddenly Last Summer, Trojan Women* (The Studios)

Television includes: *Shirley, Luther, Stolen, Casualty, Law & Order, Whistleblowers, Silent Witness.*

Film includes: *Severance, Light.*

JULIE DRAY
Mathilde

Theatre includes: *Red Light Winter* (Elephant Theatre LA); *Faux Départ* (Théâtre Rive Gauche Paris); *Jalousie en Trois Fax* (European tour); *Le Poulet est Rôti* (Tadam, Paris).

Television includes: *Land Girls, Toussaint Louverture, Camping, Doctors, Vive Les Vacances, Venus Et Appollon, Le Juge est une Femme, Douleur Muette, Si J'Avais des Millions, Une Nouvelle Vie, Julie Lescaut, La Loi du Plus Fort, Navarro, Josephine, Commissariat Bastille, Une Famille Formidable, Division d'Honneur, Méditerranée, Un Homme en Colère, Un et Un Font Six, Marc Eliot.*

Film includes: *La Vie d'une Autre, Do Elephants Pray?, Ralph, Gaga, Comme un Lundi, Mariage Mixte, Deuxième Vie.*

JACK FARTHING
Vin

Theatre includes: *Mary Broome* (Orange Tree); *Charlie's Aunt, Comedy of Errors* (Manchester Royal Exchange); *Love's Labour's Lost* (Shakespeare's Globe/US Tour); *Romeo and Juliet, Helen* (Shakespeare's Globe); *The Odyssey* (National Theatre).

Radio includes: *Dunsinane* (RSC/BBC Radio 3).

Television includes: *Pram Face* (BBC3)

Film includes: *Bright Star*

ORLA FITZGERALD
Sadhbh

Theatre includes: *The Comedy of Errors, The Playboy of the Western World* (Royal Exchange); *Dov and Ali, Crestfall* (Theatre503); *Pumpgirl* (Bush); *This Ebony Bird* (Blood in the Alley); *The System* (The Project); *The Day I Swapped My Dad for Two Goldfish* (The Ark); *A Town Called F**ked* (Last Serenade)

Macbeth (Second Age); *A Quite Life* (Peacock Theatre); *The River* (Meridian Theatre Company); *Who's Breaking* (Graffiti Theatre Company); *Laodamia* (Merlin International Theatre Co.); *Disco Pigs* (Corcadorca Theatre Co.).

Television includes: *Law & Order, Holby City, In the Company of Strangers, The Last Furlong, The Baby Wars, Love is the Bug.*

Film includes: *Speed Dating, The Wind That Shakes the Barley, Loves Elusive, Stranger in the Night.*

DAN FREDENBURGH
Stephen

Theatre includes: *Love's Labour's Lost* (Rose, Kingston); *Portrait of a Lady* (Bath/UK Tour); *A Few Good Men* (Theatre Royal Haymarket); *Children of a Lesser God* (Salisbury); *Sunday Father* (Hampstead); *Mnemonic* (International tour); *The Prince of Homburg* (RSC/Lyric); *An Inspector Calls* (Garrick); *Out in the Cold, Le Chandelier* (Greenwich Studio); *A Woman's Comedy* (Wimbledon Theatre); *Skinwalker* (BAC); *Barefoot in the Park* (Frinton Rep).

Television includes: *Casualty, Emma, Ashes To Ashes, Silent Witness, Waking the Dead, Donovan, The Bill, Holby City, Doctors* (BBC); *Lexx* (Silver Light Prods); *Bad Girls* (Granada); *Queen of Swords* (Amy Artists Int.); *Sword Of Honour* (Talkback); *The Knock* (LWT); *Douch Anglais* (Canal +).

Film includes: *The Bourne Ultimatum* (Universal Pictures); *Earthquakes* (short); *Broken Lines* (Riverchild Films); *Land Of The Blind* (Defender Film Company); *Love Actually* (Working Title Films); *Al's Lads* (Alchemy Pictures); *Café De Paris* (short); *Brothers* (Brothers Films); *The Lake District* (Plato Screen Productions); *The Sweet Rain* (Screen Ventures).

PAUL HICKEY
Michael/Ronan

For Out of Joint and the Royal Court, Paul appeared in Stella Feehily's *O Go My Man*. Other theatre includes: *Our Class, Peer Gynt, Romeo and Juliet, The Playboy of the Western World* (National Theatre); *Fewer Emergencies, Crazyblackmuthafuckinself* (Royal Court); *Ghosts* (Arcola); *Wallenstein* (Chichester); *Drink Dance Laugh and Lie* (Bush); *In A Little World of Our Own, Pentecost* (Donmar Warehouse); *Dealer's Choice, My Night With Reg* (Birmingham Rep); *The Merchant of Venice* (RSC/world tour); *The Deep Blue Sea* (Manchester Royal Exchange); *The Plough and the Stars, Aristocrats, The Silver Tassie, Howling Moons Silent Sons* (Abbey Theatre).

Television includes:
Whitechapel, Sunshine, Inspector Lynley Mysteries (Series IV, V & VI), *Nuremburg, Friends and Crocodiles, Murder City, Rebel Heart, Informant, Father Ted, The American*.

Films include: *The Matchmaker, Though the Sky Falls, On the Edge, Saving Private Ryan, Moll Flanders, Nora, Spin the Bottle, The General, Ordinary Decent Criminal*.

PENA IIYAMBO
Child Soldier/Amala/
Screaming Child

Pena has been a member of Italia Conti Stage school for three years. She is very excited about making her professional debut as Amala in Out of Joint's co-production of *Bang Bang Bang*.

AKLEIA LOUIS-FREDERICK
Child Soldier/Amala/
Screaming Child

Akleia Louis-Frederick is thirteen years old and has been a member of the Young Actors Theatre for three years. She enjoys singing and playing the piano, reading and art. Akleia is delighted to be making her professional debut as Amala in Out of Joint's production of *Bang Bang Bang*

JESSICA RICHARDSON
Child Soldier/Amala/
Screaming Child

Theatre includes: *Joseph and the Amazing Technicolour Dreamcoat* (Adelphi); *Annie Get Your Gun* (Young Vic); *Joe Turner's Come and Gone* by August Wilson and directed by David Lan (Young Vic).

GRAHAM COWLEY
Producer

Out of Joint's Producer since 1998. His long collaboration with Max Stafford-Clark began as Joint Stock Theatre Group's first General Manager for seven years in the 1970s. He was General Manager of the Royal Court for eight years, and on their behalf transferred a string of hit plays to the West End. His career has spanned the full range of theatre production, from small fringe companies to major West End shows and large scale commercial tours. Outside Out of Joint, he has translated Véronique Olmi's *End of Story* (Chelsea Theatre) and has produced the 'Forgotten Voices from the Great War' series of plays including *What the Women Did* (Southwark Playhouse, 2004), *Red Night* by James Lansdale Hodson (Finborough, 2005) and *My Real War 1914-?*, based on the letters of a young WW1 soldier, which toured twice in 2007 and played at Trafalgar Studios in October 2009. His next production is *Ex*, a new play with songs at the Soho Theatre in November 2011.

STELLA FEEHILY
Writer

Stella's stage plays include
Duck and *O Go My Man* (Out of
Joint/Royal Court); *Dreams of
Violence* (Out of Joint/ Soho
Theatre); *Catch*, written with
four other playwrights (Royal
Court); and *Game* (Fishamble
Theatre Company/Project Arts
Centre, Dublin). Radio plays
include *Sweet Bitter* (Lyric FM
in association with Fishamble)
and *Julia Roberts' Teeth* (BBC3).
She was co-winner of the
Susan Smith Blackburn Award
2007 for *O Go My Man*.

DES KENNEDY
Associate Director

Des Kennedy is originally from
Belfast. He was on the
National Theatre Studio
Directors' Course in 2010 and
has worked as an Assistant
Director under Dominic Cooke
at the Royal Court and Mike
Bradwell at the Bush.

Directing include: *The Prophet
of Monto* (Flea Theater, New
York); *JonnyMeister + the Stitch*
(Mead Theatre, Washington
DC); *The Great Ramshackle
Heart* (Old Vic New
Voices/Public Theater, New
York); *Dying City* (Project Arts
Centre, Dublin); *Seven Jewish
Children* (Queen's Studio,
Belfast); *Salaam Mr Bush!*
(rehearsed reading, Royal
Court Young Writers' Festival);
The Last Days of Judas Iscariot
(Brian Friel Theatre, Belfast);
Scenes from the Big Picture
(Callan Theatre, Washington
DC – Helen Hayes nominated
production and named one of
the best ten productions of
the decade, *Washington Post*);
The Laramie Project (National
Student Drama Festival, 2004,
Bush Theatre Directing
Award).

Des is currently Out of Joint's
Associate Director. In 2011 he
directs *How The World Began*,
in association with Out of
Joint and the Arcola Theatre.

MARK MURPHY
Movement director

Mark is an award-winning
director, writer and outdoor
event specialist. As founder of
Vtol, he directed between
1991 and 2001, seven major
international touring shows. In
the 1990s his name also
became synonymous with The
Northern Stage Ensemble –
directing *A Clockwork Orange*
and the award-winning *1984*
and in 2002 he became
associate director for outdoor
specialists Walk The Plank. He
has written three plays – *A
Wing and a Prayer*, *The Night
Shift* (world premiere at the
Traverse Theatre) and *Have a
Go Hero* and also received two
Peggy Ramsay Foundation
awards for his writing. He has
collaborated with Legs On The
Wall by writing and co-
directing their Helpmann
award winning show *On the
Case* for the Melbourne
Commonwealth Games and
has also written and directed
work for The National Theatre
of Scotland and NVA. In 2008,
he directed the opening
ceremony for the Liverpool
Capital of Culture to a live
audience of sixty thousand
and later co-wrote and
directed *Aisling's Children* in the
Esplanade of Edinburgh Castle.
Alongside Walk the Plank he
created the prestigious
opening event for Turku's
(Finland) 2011 European
Capital of Culture and has
recently been appointed
Artistic Director for the London
2012 Legacy Trust project in
Belfast. He is currently working
on a new project at Warwick
Arts Centre entitled Take A
Deep Breath (vimeo.com/mrm
arkmurphy).

MIRIAM NABARRO
Designer

Miriam is a London-based
theatre designer, photographer
and artist. Trained at Central
Saint Martins/ HKU, the
University of Edinburgh and
SOAS.

Theatre includes *The Great
Game: Afghanistan* (Tricycle

and US tour, Olivier nominated,
co-design with Pamela
Howard); *Mad Blud* (Theatre
Royal Stratford East); *The Snow
Queen* (Polka); *Prima
Doona* (Gilded Balloon/ Menier
Fringe First 2010); *The Winter's
Tale* (Headlong/Schtanhaus/
Nuffield); *Twelfth Night*,
Macbeth, *A Midsummer Night's
Dream* (all NT Primary
Classics); *The Quicken Tree*
(Botanics Productions); *Don't
Shoot the Clowns* (Fuel); *Palace
of the End* (Royal Exchange/
Traverse, Amnesty
International Award 09); *Dr
Korczak's Example* (Royal
Exchange/Arcola/MEN Best
Studio Production); *Sabbat*,
The Wonderful Wizard of Oz
(Dukes); *Tombstone*,
Tales and *George and the
Dragon* (both Schtanhaus);
Pains of Youth (RADA); *Measure
for Measure* and *ID 1000* (NYT);
Carmen (Pegasus Opera); *The
Voluptuous Tango* (Almeida
New Opera); and *The Fear
Brigade* by Adrian Mitchell. She
is currently developing a new
song cycle, *War
Correspondents* with Helen
Chadwick.

Exhibitions include *SE1 9PX:
Hidden Corners*, her solo
photographic show at the NT,
and group shows: *Dreams* at
the Freud museum, *Artisterium*
(British Council, Georgia)
and *ELP in Space*.

Miriam has worked extensively
as a community artist and
humanitarian worker for NGOs
and the British Council in
Sudan, Eritrea, Georgia, Kosova,
Iran and Syria. She spent a year
setting up psychosocial
programmes for children
affected by conflict in eastern
DRC.

ANDY SMITH
Sound Designer

Andy's sound designs include
Sweeney Todd, *Secret Thoughts*,
The Demolition Man, *The Price*,
Romeo and Juliet, *David
Copperfield*, *Love on the Dole*, *A
Streetcar Named Desire*, *The
Hired Man*, *Rafta Rafta*, *The
Comedians*, *And Did Those Feet*,
A Midsummer Night's Dream

and *Oliver Twist* (Octagon Theatre Bolton); *Mixed Up North* (Octagon Theatre Bolton/Out of Joint); *Looking for Buddy* (Octagon Theatre Bolton/Live Theatre, Newcastle); and *Blonde Bombshells of 1943* (Octagon Theatre Bolton/Hampstead Theatre).

MAX STAFFORD-CLARK
Director

Educated at Trinity College, Dublin, Max Stafford-Clark co-founded Joint Stock Theatre Group in 1974 following his Artistic Directorship of The Traverse Theatre, Edinburgh. From 1979 to 1993 he was Artistic Director of The Royal Court Theatre. In 1993 he founded the touring company, Out of Joint. His work as a director has overwhelmingly been with new writing, and he has commissioned and directed first productions by many leading writers, including Sue Townsend, Stephen Jeffreys, Timberlake Wertenbaker, Sebastian Barry, April de Angelis, Mark Ravenhill, Andrea Dunbar, Robin Soans, Alistair Beaton, Stella Feehily, David Hare and Caryl Churchill. In addition he has directed classic texts including *The Seagull, The Recruiting Officer* and *King Lear* for the Royal Court; *A Jovial Crew, The Wives' Excuse* and *The Country Wife* for The Royal Shakespeare Company; and *The Man of Mode, She Stoops to Conquer, Three Sisters* and *Macbeth* for Out of Joint. He directed David Hare's *The Breath of Life* for Sydney Theatre Company in 2003. His production of *Top Girls* for Out of Joint and Chichester Festival Theatre transferred to Trafalgar Studios in August 2011. Academic credits include honorary doctorates from Oxford Brookes, Warwick and Hertfordshire Universities and visiting professorships at the Universities of Hertfordshire, Warwick and York. His books are *Letters to George, Taking Stock* and *Our Country's Good: Page to Stage*.

JOHANNA TOWN
Lighting Designer

Johanna has previously designed numerous productions for Out of Joint including *The Overwhelming, The Permanent Way* (and Sydney) and *Our Lady of Sligo* – all Out of Joint with the National Theatre; *O Go My Man, Talking to Terrorists, Shopping and Fucking* (West End/world tour) and *The Steward of Christendom* (Brooklyn Academy of Music and Sydney Festival) – all Out of Joint with the Royal Court; *Dreams of Violence* (UK tour); *Macbeth* (World tour/Arcola) and *King of Hearts* and *Feelgood* (Hampstead). Other theatre credits include: *Betrayal, Speaking in Tongues, Fat Pig, Hello and Goodbye, Top Girls, Via Dolorosa, Beautiful Thing* (West End); *Rose* (National/Broadway); *My Name is Rachel Corrie* (Royal Court/West End/New York); *Guantanamo Bay* (Tricycle/West End/New York); *Re-Charged* (Soho); *Fatherland* (Gate); *The Pride, That Face* (Sheffield Crucible); *Beautiful Thing, A View from the Bridge, Haunted* (also Brits off Broadway and Australia); *Private Lives, A Raisin in the Sun, The Glass Menagerie* (Manchester Royal Exchange); *The Game of Love and Chance, Les Liaisons Dangereuses* and *The Herbal Bed* (Salisbury); *Romeo and Juliet, The Importance of Being Earnest* (Royal Lyceum, Edinburgh); *Pride and Prejudice* (tour); *The Tragedy of Thomas Hobbes* (RSC); *Llwyth* (tour); *For King and Country* (tour); *Mad Forest* (BAC); *The Hounding of David Oluwale* (WYP/tour); *Pirates, The Ride of Your Life* (Polka); *Badenheim 1939, Tipping the Velvet, City of Angels, Damn Yankees* (Guildhall); *Small Craft Warnings* (Arcola); *Dead Funny, To Kill a Mockingbird* (WYP); *The Deep Blue Sea/Nijinsky, In Praise of Love* (Chichester Festival Theatre); *ID* (Almeida/BBC); and numerous productions for the Royal Court including *Faces in the Crowd, The Arsonists, Rhinoceros, My Child.*

Opera includes productions for Scottish opera, Classical Opera, Nice Opera House, Opera 80, Almeida Opera Festival and Music Theatre London.

KAMAU WA NDUNG'U
Assistant Director

Born and raised in Mathare slum, Nairobi, Kamau has been an actor and a director for more than ten years.

Stage appearances include: *Sarafina, Luanda Magere, An Enemy of the People, Richard III, Othello, Dead Man's Hand, Run For Your Wife.*

Films include: *The First Grader, The Hunting of Dedan Kimathi, The Bush Fire, The Dose, Poison.*

Television includes: *Reflections, Asali,* and *Heartbeat FM* (Kenyan)

As Creative Coordinator Kamau oversees the artistic output of SAFE, running training workshops, heading up SAFE's forum theatre intervention, and co-directing and devising original performance pieces.

In December 2008, during my second time working as a reporter for the _Irish Times_ in Eastern DRC, a moment of culinary surrealism among the drunken soldiers and the child killers caught me by surprise.

In Lushebere farm, about six kilometres outside the commercial centre of Masisi in North Kivu, I watched as Muda Hikiamana wrapped two rounds of cheese and examined forensically the $5 dollar note handed to him. I'd stumbled upon one of the remotest commercial cheesemakers in the world. He also happened to be operating his business in the middle of a war zone, surrounded by four different militias and thousands of displaced persons. Through a local contact, I'd been told to wait there for General Edmo Gandi, from the FDLR militia group, one of the most feared and despised rebel groups in existence, made up of some of the perpetrators of the Rwandan genocide in 1994 when one million Rwandan nationals were killed. In any circumstances, it would have been bad manners to leave without sampling the produce. Behind several disused buildings, Muda, the cheesemaker opened up a large store room where hundreds of rounds of Goude cheese were stored in rusting shelves, ready for shipment all over central Africa.

The factory had been there since 1974, and the land was leased from the local clergy, who took a sizeable chunk of his profits in return. In so far as possible, the business had operated from then until now, despite the continuous cycles of violence that have raged in this province of Eastern Congo. In the late 1990s, following large influx of Hutu fighters from Rwanda, many of whom would later form the Forces Democratiques de Liberation du Rwanda (FDLR), the factory ceased production, re-starting again in 2001. There were temporary stoppages also when the Congrès national pour la défense du peuple (CNDP) – the band of mainly Tutsi militia under the command of renegade General Laurent Nkunda – made advances in the region in recent years. 'My grandfather and my whole family worked in this factory,' Muda told me. 'Thankfully the machines have not been stolen following each round of fighting so we have been able to re-start. From here, the cheese goes to Goma, and then onto Rwanda, Kinshasa, Uganda and all over Africa.'

When I visited in 2008, Masisi was under the control of the Congolese army (FARDC), the FDLR and various other local militias, while the UN's MONUC force also maintained a battalion on a hillside overlooking the area. At night, rifle fire could be heard on the hillsides outside our compound and the army were a largely inebriated and ill-disciplined bunch, in contrast to the rebels, who could be seen marching through the streets at dawn training child soldiers. Fourteen-year-olds in Eminem T-shirts and Nike runners manned border crossings or carried RPGs through the forests. There was a _Mad Max_ feel to the whole area – at one point a sixty-kilometre journey took two days to complete, such were the security concerns.

Cheesemaker Muda told me, proudly, there were ten employees working for Goude cheeses, producing one hundred and five rolls a week, which generated revenues of $2000 a month. Like any obsessive food producer, when I asked Muda what ingredients made his cheese so sought after, he remained tight-lipped, 'Ah, that is a professional secret,' he said. I casually remarked that Ireland did alright on the cheese front too. 'Ours though is the better quality.'

The real reason for me to be at this farm was not to sample cheese but to try get an insight into the minds of the rebel commanders and conduct a face-to-face interview. It was, in hindsight, a precarious position, and we had to make a judgement on whether or not our contact was trustworthy when he said the rebels would speak to us and guarantee our safety. As we chatted, my driver pointed in the direction of a laneway where we'd come from. Three khaki dressed rebels with AK-47s spread out along the road, and signalled for us to shadow them down a narrow path.

I was conscious too that I was about to shake hands with one of several manifestations of evil operating in this perpetually aggressive part of the world. These rebels had fled Rwanda after the genocide, many of them having committed horrendous multiple acts of murder. They were now involved in a proxy war the world had continued to ignore, and which still raged over a decade on. I wanted to know what his role was in the Rwanda genocide and whether it was true the rebels were now being funded by other African states with vested interests in an unstable Democratic Republic of Congo.

So, what does a killer look like? The ironically named General Gandi was wearing a Bush Tucker Man type hat and carried a large walking stick. He was well fed, attentive and thorough. Before sitting down on a grass embankment, he asked for a list of questions, which he then methodically went through. Most he answered in a roundabout way. His forces were fighting to be allowed back to Rwanda and their struggle went back as far as the 1970s he stated. 'The Rwandan government's goal,' he said, 'is to come and conquer North and East Kivu. They are interested only in diamonds and gold.'

We talked at length – he even posed for photographs. His English was impeccable and he reiterated over and over that he was simply a freedom fighter caught up in a struggle for land. His people were displaced. His role was to lead them home.

Only two questions he wouldn't answer – who funded his rebel group, and why exactly did he have to leave Rwanda so abruptly in the 1990s?

Brian O'Connell

Brian O'Connell is an *Irish Times* journalist, author and broadcaster.

Timeline: Democratic Republic of Congo

A Chronology of Key Events

1200s Rise of Kongo empire, centred in modern northern Angola and including extreme western Congo and territories round lakes Kisale and Upemba in central Katanga (now Shaba).

1482 Portuguese navigator Diogo Cao becomes the first European to visit the Congo; Portuguese set up ties with the king of Kongo.

16th–17th centuries British, Dutch, Portuguese and French merchants engage in slave trade through Kongo intermediaries.

1870s Belgian King Leopold II sets up a private venture to colonise Kongo.

1874-77 British explorer Henry Stanley navigates Congo river to the Atlantic Ocean.

Belgian Colonisation

1879–87 Leopold commissions Stanley to establish the king's authority in the Congo basin.

1884–85 European powers at the Conference of Berlin recognise Leopold's claim to the Congo basin.

1885 Leopold announces the establishment of the Congo Free State, headed by himself.

1891-92 Belgians conquer Katanga.

1892–94 Eastern Congo wrested from the control of East African Arab and Swahili-speaking traders.

1908 Belgian state annexes Congo amid protests over killings and atrocities carried out on a mass scale by Leopold's agents. Millions of Congolese are said to have been killed or worked to death during Leopold's control of the territory.

1955 Belgian Professor Antoin van Bilsen publishes a '30-Year Plan' for granting the Congo increased self-government.

1959 Belgium begins to lose control over events in the Congo following serious nationalist riots in Leopoldville (now Kinshasa).

Post-Independence Turmoil

1960 June – Congo becomes independent with Patrice Lumumba as prime minister and Joseph Kasavubu as president.

1960 July – Congolese army mutinies; Moise Tshombe declares Katanga independent; Belgian troops sent in ostensibly to protect Belgian citizens and mining interests; UN Security Council votes to send in troops to help establish order, but the troops are not allowed to intervene in internal affairs.

1960 September – Kasavubu dismisses Lumumba as prime minister.

1960 December – Lumumba arrested.

1961 February – Lumumba murdered, reportedly with US and Belgian complicity.

1961 August – UN troops begin disarming Katangese soldiers.

1963 – Tshombe agrees to end Katanga's secession.

1964 – President Kasavubu appoints Tshombe prime minister.

Mobutu Years

1965 – Kasavubu and Tshombe ousted in a coup led by Joseph Mobutu.

1971 – Joseph Mobutu renames the country Zaire and himself Mobutu Sese Seko; also Katanga becomes Shaba and the river Congo becomes the river Zaire.

1973–74 – Mobutu nationalises many foreign-owned firms and forces European investors out of the country.

1977 – Mobutu invites foreign investors back, without much success; French, Belgian and Moroccan troops help repulse attack on Katanga by Angolan-based rebels.

1989 – Zaire defaults on loans from Belgium, resulting in a cancellation of development programmes and increased deterioration of the economy.

1990 – Mobutu agrees to end the ban on multiparty politics and appoints a transitional government, but retains substantial powers.

1991 – Following riots in Kinshasa by unpaid soldiers, Mobutu agrees to a coalition government with opposition leaders, but retains control of the security apparatus and important ministries.

1993 – Rival pro- and anti-Mobutu governments created.

1994 – Mobutu agrees to the appointment of Kengo Wa Dondo, an advocate of austerity and free-market reforms, as prime minister.

1996-97 – Tutsi rebels capture much of eastern Zaire while Mobutu is abroad for medical treatment.

Aftermath of Mobutu

1997 May – Tutsi and other anti-Mobutu rebels, aided principally by Rwanda, capture the capital, Kinshasa; Zaire is renamed the Democratic Republic of Congo; Laurent-Desire Kabila installed as president.

1998 August – Rebels backed by Rwanda and Uganda rise up against Kabila and advance on Kinshasa. Zimbabwe, Namibia send troops to repel them. Angolan troops also side with Kabila. The rebels take control of much of the east of DR Congo.

1999 – Rifts emerge between Congolese Liberation Movement (MLC) rebels supported by Uganda and Rally for Congolese Democracy (RCD) rebels backed by Rwanda.

Lusaka Peace Accord Signed

1999 July – The six African countries involved in the war sign a ceasefire accord in Lusaka. The following month the MLC and RCD rebel groups sign the accord.

2000 – UN Security Council authorises a 5,500-strong UN force to monitor the ceasefire but fighting continues between rebels and government forces, and between Rwandan and Ugandan forces.

2001 January – President Laurent Kabila is shot dead by a bodyguard. Joseph Kabila succeeds his father.

2001 February – Kabila meets Rwandan President Paul Kagame in Washington. Rwanda, Uganda and the rebels agree to a UN pull-out plan. Uganda, Rwanda begin pulling troops back from the frontline.

2001 May – US refugee agency says the war has killed 2.5 million people, directly or indirectly, since August 1998. Later, a UN panel says the warring parties are deliberately prolonging the conflict to plunder gold, diamonds, timber and coltan, used in the making of mobile phones.

2002 January – Eruption of Mount Nyiragongo devastates much of the city of Goma.

Search for Peace

2002 April – Peace talks in South Africa: Kinshasa signs a power-sharing deal with Ugandan-backed rebels, under which the MLC leader would be premier. Rwandan-backed RCD rebels reject the deal.

2002 July – Presidents of DR Congo and Rwanda sign a peace deal under which Rwanda will withdraw troops from the east and DR Congo will disarm and arrest Rwandan Hutu gunmen blamed for the killing of the Tutsi minority in Rwanda's 1994 genocide.

2002 September – Presidents of DR Congo and Uganda sign peace accord under which Ugandan troops will leave DR Congo.

2002 September/October – Uganda, Rwanda say they have withdrawn most of their forces from the east. UN-sponsored power-sharing talks begin in South Africa.

2002 December – Peace deal signed in South Africa between Kinshasa government and main rebel groups. Under the deal rebels and opposition members are to be given portfolios in an interim government.

Interim Government

2003 April – President Kabila signs a transitional constitution, under which an interim government will rule pending elections.

2003 May – Last Ugandan troops leave eastern DR Congo.

2003 June – French soldiers arrive in Bunia, spearheading a UN-mandated rapid-reaction force.

2003 President Kabila names a transitional government to lead until elections in two years time. Leaders of main former rebel groups are sworn in as vice-presidents in July.

2003 August – Interim parliament inaugurated.

2004 March – Gunmen attack military bases in Kinshasa in an apparent coup attempt.

2004 June – Reported coup attempt by rebel guards is said to have been neutralised.

2004 December – Fighting in the east between the Congolese army and renegade soldiers from a former pro-Rwanda rebel group. Rwanda denies being behind the mutiny.

2005 March – UN peacekeepers say they have killed more then 50 militia members in an offensive, days after nine Bangladeshi soldiers serving with the UN are killed in the north-east.

New Constitution

2005 May – New constitution, with text agreed by former warring factions, is adopted by parliament.

2005 September – Uganda warns that its troops may re-enter DR Congo after a group of Ugandan Lord's Resistance Army rebels enter via Sudan.

2005 November – A first wave of soldiers from the former Zairean army returns after almost eight years of exile in the neighbouring Republic of Congo.

2005 December – Voters back a new constitution, already approved by parliament, paving the way for elections in 2006.

International Court of Justice rules that Uganda must compensate DR Congo for rights abuses and the plundering of resources in the five years up to 2003.

2006 February – New constitution comes into force; new national flag is adopted.

2006 March – Warlord Thomas Lubanga becomes first war crimes suspect to face charges at the International Criminal Court in The Hague. He is accused of forcing children into active combat.

2006 May – Thousands are displaced in the north-east as the army and UN peacekeepers step up their drive to disarm irregular forces ahead of the elections.

Free Elections

2006 July – Presidential and parliamentary polls are held – the first free elections in four decades. With no clear winner in the presidential vote, incumbent leader Joseph Kabila and opposition candidate Jean-Pierre Bemba prepare to contest a run-off poll on 29 October. Forces loyal to the two candidates clash in the capital.

2006 November – Joseph Kabila is declared winner of October's run-off presidential election. The poll has the general approval of international monitors.

2006 December – Forces of renegade General Laurent Nkunda and the UN-backed army clash in North Kivu province, prompting some 50,000 people to flee. The UN Security Council expresses concern about the fighting.

2007 March – Government troops and forces loyal to opposition leader Jean-Pierre Bemba clash in Kinshasa.

2007 April – DR Congo, Rwanda and Burundi relaunch the regional economic bloc Great lakes Countries Economic Community, known under its French acronym CEPGL.

2007 April – Jean-Pierre Bemba leaves for Portugal, ending a three-week political stalemate in Kinshasa, during which he sheltered in the South African embassy.

2007 May – The UN investigates allegations of gold and arms trafficking by UN peacekeepers in Ituri region.

2007 June – War could break out again in the east, warns the Archbishop of Bukavu, Monsignor Francois-Xavier Maroy.

2007 June – Radio Okapi broadcaster Serge Maheshe is shot dead in Bukavu, the third journalist killed in the country since 2005.

2007 Augus – Uganda and DR Congo agree to try defuse a border dispute.

2007 – Aid agencies report a big increase in refugees fleeing instability in North Kivu which is blamed on dissident general Nkunda.

2007 September – Major outbreak of the deadly Ebola virus.

2008 January – The government and rebel militia, including renegade Gen Nkunda, sign a peace pact aimed at ending years of conflict in the east.

Renewed Clashes

2008 April – Army troops clash with Rwandan Hutu militias with whom they were formerly allied in eastern Congo, leaving thousands of people displaced.

2008 Augus – Heavy clashes erupt in the east of the country between army troops and fighters loyal to rebel leader Laurent Nkunda.

2008 October – Rebel forces capture major army base of Rumangabo; the Congolese government accuses Rwanda of backing General Nkunda, a claim Rwanda denies.

2008 Thousands of people, including Congolese troops, flee as clashes in eastern DR Congo intensify. Chaos grips the provincial capital Goma as rebel forces advance. UN peacekeepers engage the rebels in an attempt to support Congolese troops.

2008 November – Campaign by Tutsi rebel leader Laurent Nkunda to consolidate control over east prompts new wave of refugees.

2008 UN Security Council approves temporary increase of troops to bolster the strained UN peacekeeping effort.

2008 December – Uganda, South Sudan and DRCongo launch joint assault on Ugandan Lord's Resistance Army bases in north-east DR Congo. Hundreds of civilians are killed in backlash attacks.

2009 January – Launch of joint DR Congo-Rwandan military operation against Tutsi rebels led by Laurent Nkunda. Campaign lasts five weeks.

Nkunda is displaced by Bosco Ntaganda and arrested in Rwanda.

2009 February – Médecins San Frontières accuses UN peacekeepers of failing to protect civilians from LRA rebels.

2009 April – Hutu militia re-emerge after end of joint DR Congo-Rwanda campaign in east, prompting thousands to flee.

2009 May – Kabila approves law giving amnesty to armed groups as part of deal meant to end fighting in east.

2009 June – International Criminal Court orders ex-vice president Jean-Pierre Bemba to stand trial on charges of war crimes for his troops' actions in Central African Republic between 2002 and 2003.

Series of mutinies by soldiers in the east complaining they haven't been paid.

2009 July – Swiss court rules that frozen assets of ex-president Mobutu Sese Seko be returned to his family.

2009 August – US Secretary of State Hillary

Clinton visits Goma, promises $17 million aid for victims of sexual violence.

Head of MONUC Alan Doss declares five months of joint army-UN operations against Rwandan rebels – "Kimia 2" – to have been "largely positive".

2009 September – UN High Commissioner for Human Rights Navi Pillay suspects October–November 2008 violence in North Kivu may amount to war crimes committed by both the army and CNDP militia.

2009 November – Germany arrests two alleged FDLR leaders on suspicion of war crimes in eastern DR Congo.

2009 December – UN extends mandate of MONUC for shortened five months, as a step to full withdrawal by mid-2010.

2010 May – Government steps up pressure for UN peacekeepers to quit before elections in 2011. UN's top humanitarian official John Holmes warns against premature departure.

2010 June – Prominent human rights advocate Floribert Chebeya found dead a day after being summoned to meet the chief of police.

Celebrations mark 50 years of independence.

2010 July – $8 billion debt relief deal approved by World Bank and IMF.

New electoral commission launched to prepare for 2011 elections.

2010 July–August – Mass rapes reported in North Kivu province. UN envoy Margot Wallstrom blames both rebels and army.

2010 June–August – Operation Rwenzori against Ugandan ADF-NALU rebels prompts 90,000 to flee in North Kivu province.

2010 October – UN report into killing of Hutus in DR Congo between 1993 and 2003 says they may constitute "crimes of genocide". It implicates Rwanda, Uganda, Burundi, Zimbabwe and Angola.

2010 November – UN agencies report widespread rapes during mass expulsion of illegal migrants from Angola to DRCongo.

UN report accuses networks within army of promoting violence in east to profit from mining, smuggling and poaching.

Ex-DR Congo vice-president Jean-Pierre Bemba goes on trial at International Criminal Court accused of letting his troops rape and kill in Central African Republic between 2002 and 2003.

Paris Club of creditor countries scrap half of DR Congo's debt.

2011 January – Constitution changed, which some say boost President Kabila's election chances.

2011 February – Court sentences Lt-Col Kibibi Mutware to 20 years in jail in a mass rape case in eastern Congo. This is the first conviction of a commanding officer for rape in eastern DR Congo.

19 killed in coup bid against president, police say.

2011 May – Rwandan Hutu rebel Ignace Murwanashyaka goes on trial in Germany for alleged crimes against humanity in DR Congo.

BANG BANG BANG

Stella Feehily

For Anneke, Miriam, Max.

Acknowledgements

My grateful thanks to:

Dominic Cooke, Mel Kenyon, Ruth Little, Rachel Taylor, Nic Wass, Graham Cowley, John Blackmore, Patrick Sandford, Miriam Nabarro, Gerard Feehily, Paul Hickey, Giles Cooper, Lucy Briars, Babou Ceesay, Aoife McMahon, Mickey Sumner, Mia Soteriou, Mel Corker, Brian O'Connell, Nigel and Hilary Stafford-Clark, Claudia Seymore, Zoe Marriage, Ann McFerran, Anneke Van Woudenberg, Tom Porteous, Daniel Nelson, Gaby Smith, Aisling Swaine, David Thacker, Philip Wilson, Ian Gilly, Amy Ball, Lotte Hines, Veronique Aubert, Scilla Ellworthy, Victoria Brittain, Mike Dixon, Olivia Blanchard, Anna Wilkins, Mohamed Osman, Marcus Bleasdale, Susanna Bennett, Lucy Ashken, Vickiesha Chabra, Chris Jameson, Jon Bradfield, Panda Cox, Chantelle Staynings, Chris Campbell, Kamau Wa Ndung'u, Steve Crawshaw, Emily McLoughlin, Des Kennedy.

And as ever – to Max Stafford-Clark – more than a legend in his own lunchtime.

S.F.
July 2011

French translation by Miriam Nabarro
Swahili translation by Charles Mampasu

Note on the Text

A forward slash (/) in the text indicates the point at which the next speaker interrupts.

This text went to press before the end of rehearsals and so may differ slightly from the play as performed.

Characters

In order of appearance

SADHBH, *Irish, twenty-nine*
MATHILDE, *French, twenties*
SOLDIER, *Congolese, twenties*
STEPHEN, *English, late thirties*
BIBI, *American, late thirties*
CHILD SOLDIER
WOMAN WITH SICK BABY
MAMA CAROLINA
AMALA, *nine*
FEMALE SOLDIER
COLONEL MBURAME, *twenties*
RONAN, *thirty*
VIN, *twenty-three*
INNOCENT
SCREAMING CHILD
MICHAEL, *thirties*

Doubling:

Sadhbh (pronounced 'Sigh-ve')
Stephen
Amala / Child Soldier / Screaming Child
Bibi / Mother with sick baby / Mama Carolina / Female soldier
Mathilde
Soldier / Colonel Mburame / Innocent
Ronan / Michael
Vin

PROLOGUE

The DDH compound. North Kivu.

Democratic Republic of Congo.

NGO – (Pour La Défense des Droits des Hommes.) DDH.

June.

Sand and dirt floor. Plastic chairs and crates shoved against a door. Outside the compound gunfire crackles – a kind of chaos is gathering. Some high windows let in light.

Threatening shadows against the back wall.

Two Human Rights defenders – SADHBH and MATHILDE are huddled together.

MATHILDE. *Je veux Maman.*
  Je veux parler à ma mère.

SADHBH. Where is your phone?

MATHILDE. On the kitchen table.

SADHBH. *C'est très dangereux, trop dangereux. Attend –*

MATHILDE. I need to tell her – I need to talk to her – in case.

SADHBH. Mathilde.

MATHILDE. It is nearly one hour and still –

  The gunfire crackle gets closer.

  Ca se rapproche.

SADHBH. *Ca vient d'où?*

MATHILDE. Closer. Closer.
  Are they in the compound? Do you?

SADHBH. Maybe not. Where did Vin go?

MATHILDE. He left the compound.

SADHBH. *Pourquoi?* Has he got our transport? Did Janvier take him somewhere?

MATHILDE. I don't know. I don't know. I don't want to be raped.

SADHBH. It's okay.

MATHILDE. *Je préfère mourir plutôt que d'être violé.*

SADHBH. *Ça va aller, ça va aller.*

The gunfire – loud and frightening – is now very close.

There are shouts of panic.

That's Janvier.

MATHILDE (*whispers*). They're in the compound.

SADHBH. Janvier has a gun.
The nearest safe room –

MATHILDE. Oxfam. We'd have to run across the courtyard.

There are shouts and a shot.

Jésus, Jésus, Jésus. Ils ont tué Janvier?

A walkie-talkie clicks into life.

SADHBH. I'll get the radio.

MATHILDE. *Me quitte pas. Me quitte pas.*

SADHBH. It's just outside the door.
Mathilde? Don't go into shock. Pull back.
I need to talk to you. Can we be calm?

MATHILDE. Okay. Okay. Okay.

SADHBH. Good girl.
How much money have you got?

MATHILDE. About nine hundred dollars.

SADHBH. I have three thousand dollars in my travel bag, which is under my bed.

MATHILDE. We've got five cartons of cigarettes here.

SADHBH. Two bottles of whiskey.

MATHILDE. Passports.

SADHBH. Phones. Our phones. My laptop. Okay?

MATHILDE. Okay.

SADHBH. We give them everything.

MATHILDE. How many are they?

SADHBH. I can only hear one, two voices.
    Maybe only two at most?

MATHILDE. Jewellery.

SADHBH. Okay? We give them everything and we talk to them.

MATHILDE. *Je ne veux pas.*

SADHBH. We talk to them. Humanise yourself.

MATHILDE. *Non. Ne les laisses pas. Je ne veux pas.*

SADHBH. Mathilde? Listen to me.
    You keep them talking but tell them you are a married
    woman. You tell them you are a mother.

MATHILDE. This can't be real.

SADHBH. You talk about God.
    You tell them they won't be damned if they leave now.
    You talk about Jesus. This is what you have got to do.
    Let me get the radio.

The door is kicked. Once. Twice.

The boxes, chairs and crates scatter. A YOUNG MAN *in
army fatigues and jeans enters. He is wearing a baseball hat.
His nose and mouth are covered with a bandanna. He is
jittery and hyped.*

Mon Dieu, pitié.

SOLDIER. *La ferme.*

SADHBH. *Je m'appelle Sadhbh, et ça c'est Mathilde.*
Nous avons de l'argent. Beaucoup des dollars.
Je vous en prie!

MATHILDE. *Nous avons des cigarettes.*

SADHBH. *Prenez tout.*

SOLDIER. *Mettez vous par terre. Tout de suite.*
Accroupies!

The SOLDIER *knocks everything across the room – kicking the boxes, crates, chairs.*

SADHBH. *Nous avons du whiskey. Prenez-le. Prenez-le, buvez le avec vos enfants.*

SOLDIER. *Déshabillez-vous.*

MATHILDE. *Non, non, je vous en prie. Nous sommes mariées.*
Nous sommes mères.

The SOLDIER *pokes the gun towards* SADHBH's *face.*

SOLDIER. *Déshabillez-vous.*

MATHILDE. *Non, non, non!*

SADHBH. *Je peux vous donner l'argent.*
Nous avons presque quatre mille dollars.
Prenez-le. C'est pour vous.
Dieu vous pardonnera, si vous partez maintenant.

SOLDIER. *Je prends l'argent.*
Je prends les téléphones.
Je prends tout.
Et, ensuite, je vais terminer le boulot.

The SOLDIER *points the gun.*

MATHILDE *starts to cry.*

The women begin to undress. They huddle together to hide their bodies.

On ne vous entend pas.
Personne ne vous écoute.

The light fades. The shadows close in.

ACT ONE

One

London.

An apartment in Holloway.

End of April.

Late Morning.

SADHBH *enters with an armful of clothes and books.*
STEPHEN, *her boyfriend, is looking at some printed material
while eating a doughnut and drinking coffee. There is a
rucksack nearby. A Stetson-like hat hangs from it. She carefully
packs the rucksack.*

SADHBH. Stephen?
   I bet we made a baby this morning.
   Hey?

   He looks up at her.

   If it's a girl I'm calling her Saoirse.

STEPHEN. Saoirse?

SADHBH. Means freedom.
   She'll not have your fat arse but she will have my legs. And
   she'll be beautiful like you but clever like me.

   She pulls out a T-shirt from the pile of clothes.

STEPHEN. What are you doing with my T-shirt?

SADHBH (*smells the T-shirt*). To… remind me.

   STEPHEN *watches her shove his T-shirt in her rucksack. He
   dunks his doughnut.*

   SADHBH *sits opposite him and starts up her laptop.*

That's going to break off.

He eats the doughnut.

You can't saturate it and expect it to taste good.

STEPHEN. It does taste good.

SADHBH. Some of it's at the bottom of your cup.

STEPHEN. You distracted me.

SADHBH. I distracted you?

STEPHEN *scoops the doughnut from his cup with a spoon and eats it.*

We hear shouting from off.

Is there more coffee?

STEPHEN. Sit.

He pours coffee.

We hear a muffled argument through the walls.

SADHBH. Did you hear?

STEPHEN. What's he said?

SADHBH. Fucking – (*Makes grunting noises.*)

A muffled crash.

Should we say something?

STEPHEN *knocks on the table.*

STEPHEN. Oh, hello. I can hear you call each other all the bastards under the sun. Would you mind awfully keeping it down?

SADHBH. To the concierge. I meant.

STEPHEN. What can he do?

SADHBH. He could tell them that they can be heard.
You know?
And say if it's more than *just* an argument?

STEPHEN. It's flat life, Sadhbh. Music, cisterns, sex –

Messy lives.

The argument stops as abruptly as it started.

Do you hear that?

SADHBH. What?

STEPHEN Maelstrom over.

SADHBH *listens.*

SADHBH. You're right.

STEPHEN. If you were here for longer than a week
you'd understand the rhythm of flat life.

SADHBH. The rhythm of flat life?

STEPHEN. He's not killing her, Sadhbh. This is Islington. Or
so the estate agent said.

SADHBH. Yeah? Well, he meant Holloway.
The rhythm of flat life?

SADHBH *returns to her laptop.*

Why are you cross with me?

STEPHEN *shrugs.*

You are cross with me?
You?
Why?

Pause.

STEPHEN *indicates the rucksack with his thumb.*

SADHBH *gets up from her chair – takes the hat off the
rucksack – puts it on and removes the rucksack from sight.*

She re-enters.

STEPHEN. You're not going –

SADHBH. Right.

STEPHEN. – till Monday.

SADHBH. I don't even know why I –

Right.

They look at one another. STEPHEN *resumes reading documents.*

How's the Mandarin going?

STEPHEN. *Ni hao!*
Qîng césuo zai nar?
Hello. Where is the toilet please?

SADHBH. All you need really.

She starts tapping the keys on her laptop.

Did *she* understand 'the rhythm of flat life'?

Pause.

STEPHEN *looks at* SADHBH.

She resumes work at her laptop.

STEPHEN. Do you want to tell me about your lovers?
That Irish Foreign Correspondent – /
Ronan What's-his-name?

SADHBH. Are you crazy? I've never been with Ronan Fitzgerald.
He's fucked everything from here to Bujumbura.

STEPHEN. I should never have told you.

SADHBH stretches out her hand to him. He puts it against his cheek. She pulls her hand away.

SADHBH (*picks up his remaining half of doughnut*). This is how you dunk a doughnut. Dunk, eat, drink.

She does so.

STEPHEN. What makes you a doughnut-dunk expert?

SADHBH. I had a scene with an aid worker from New York.

STEPHEN. When was this?

SADHBH. Way, way, way, before you.

STEPHEN. Oh yes?

SADHBH. He was very particular about dunking.

STEPHEN. I'm not sure I want any –

SADHBH. As you wish.

STEPHEN. – more information.

Pause.

SADHBH. Did she mind that you had a partner?

Pause.

Answer me.

STEPHEN. She didn't say that exactly.

SADHBH. What did she say?

STEPHEN. I can't remember.

SADHBH. Convenient.

STEPHEN. Truth.
She knew I was with you – obviously.

SADHBH. Why obviously?

STEPHEN *proffers the bag of doughnuts.*

STEPHEN. Breakfast?

She takes a doughnut.

I didn't promise anything.

SADHBH. Seeing someone over a sustained period is a promise.

STEPHEN. Not to me.

SADHBH. For you it was a series of one-night stands?

STEPHEN. Well, yes.

SADHBH. Over three months?
Interesting moral code.

She takes a bite of her doughnut.

Did she talk about the future?

STEPHEN. I don't know what you mean.

SADHBH. The relationship?
Did she think you'd leave me?

STEPHEN. She couldn't possibly have.

SADHBH. Why 'couldn't she possibly have'?

STEPHEN. We didn't have particularly in-depth conversations
about who thought what and –

SADHBH. So – now you're saying – ?

He dunks his doughnut.

STEPHEN. Look, can we drop it?

SADHBH. I want to know the facts. /
I don't want her –

STEPHEN. The facts are you're here.
You won't / ever meet her.

SADHBH. – having stuff over me.

STEPHEN. I never think of –
Can we drop it, please? Please?

SADHBH. No.

STEPHEN. The facts are you were away for eight months last
year. I missed you. I was lonely.
I'd very much like my girlfriend to live in the same country
as me.

SADHBH. The facts are you screwed someone.

She dunks her doughnut.

What's that you said?

STEPHEN. I didn't say anything.

SADHBH. The facts are you took a job at Shell.

STEPHEN. Fuck it, Sadhbh.

SADHBH. Sore point?

STEPHEN. I am a consultant on humanitarian issues for a risk-management group. Shell is a client. So shoot me.

SADHBH. You've gone over to the dark side.

STEPHEN. We can't both live on an NGO wage.

SADHBH. Such horseshit. I can live on very little –

STEPHEN. Horseshit? I'm paying the bills here.

SADHBH. It's you who –

STEPHEN. The fact is – you're about to go to the DRC for three months whether I like it or not.

SADHBH. You're going to China.

STEPHEN. For ten days.
I can't compete with your work.

SADHBH. Stephen. That's neither true nor fair.

STEPHEN. Horseshit.

SADHBH. No – it's that I can't cope with your work.
Can you see me hanging out with your Shell cronies?
Hey – there's a thought – I could lobby them at cocktail parties.

STEPHEN. I wouldn't mind that.

SADHBH. Lookit, [Now, look here,] Stephen.

STEPHEN. No. You look.
You know those women who prop up bars in Goma – who get stuck traipsing round the world's shitholes.

SADHBH. That is not going to happen to me.

STEPHEN shrugs.

I'm twenty-nine.

STEPHEN. Nearly thirty

SADHBH. And don't say 'the world's shitholes'.

STEPHEN. Have you got a –

SADHBH. That's someone's home you're talking about.

STEPHEN. – a plan? I'd like to hear it.
    Because I don't want to be the oldest dad in the playground.

SADHBH. Why do I have to change my life?

STEPHEN. Don't they teach biology in Donegal?

SADHBH. Lovers shouldn't pressure one another.

STEPHEN. Have you just swallowed a shrink?

SADHBH. Come on – you understand the work –

STEPHEN. The lack of contact, the anxiety – where are you –
    what's happening, yada yada and you – every trip – you
    become more beat, / more guilty, more – more –

SADHBH. Okay. Okay. Okay. It's stressful for you. I
    understand. Okay.
    Your pain. Your pain. / Your pain.

STEPHEN. I'm done with –

SADHBH. Okay.

STEPHEN. I'm done with arguing.
    Find a reason not to go.

SADHBH. Impossible.

STEPHEN. Think.

SADHBH. People are expecting me.
    Too many reasons why I can't –

STEPHEN. For once – think like a human being not like a
    humanitarian.

SADHBH. How can I do that?

    Silence.

STEPHEN *picks up his jacket and gathers his papers. He makes to leave.*

SADHBH. Stephen?

STEPHEN *turns around.*

STEPHEN. You said you wanted to settle.
It's why I bought the flat. 'Bambinos and all that shit' – /
that's what you said.

SADHBH. It's not for the want of trying. I defy anybody in this block of flats to say they are fucking more than we are.

STEPHEN. Then we're back to the same old – maybe if you were here for longer than a month, et cetera. And we've already covered that ground.

He puts on his jacket.

SADHBH. Are you going to the office?

STEPHEN. For a couple of hours.

SADHBH. It's Saturday.

STEPHEN. Your point?

SADHBH. Bibi is coming at seven.

STEPHEN. I'm picking up pizzas. I know.

He takes off her hat.

He kisses her. She holds him tightly until he returns her affection.

She holds him away.

SADHBH. And Bibi is a vegetarian.

STEPHEN. I know this. I also know you're taking on her work. You also know I don't like it – but who listens to a fucking word I say.

SADHBH. She's bringing the intern. Mathilde. Who will travel with me.

STEPHEN. Oh yes?

SADHBH. She's young and very pretty.
  Just – don't stare.

STEPHEN. I don't stare.

SADHBH. You stare.

STEPHEN. So kick me.

SADHBH. I will.

  He places her hat back on her head.

STEPHEN. You're not around to kick me regularly. That's the
  problem.

  STEPHEN *prepares to leave.*

SADHBH. Try not to run the work down.

  He gives her a look and exits. She calls after him.

  Stephen? I couldn't do this without you.
  And having this home to come back to –

  He calls back.

STEPHEN. It's a home – correct – not a runway.

SADHBH. Screw you.
  Screw you.

Two

Nine o'clock that evening. MATHILDE, BIBI, SADHBH,
STEPHEN. *They are all drinking and eating pizza.*

SADHBH *tops up* BIBI's *wine glass.*

MATHILDE *is pecking at a slice of pizza.*

SADHBH. Do you remember? Very early on – what you said to
  me?

BIBI. 'Stop fucking crying'?

   BIBI *takes a bite of pizza.*

SADHBH. No. Yes, you did say that – but you said – 'All of us are here for a reason – we're running away.'

BIBI. So?

SADHBH. Weren't you running from New York and your family?

BIBI. You've met most of 'em.
   So you know you thought right.

SADHBH. Sorry. Can't see you happy as a UN desk monkey.

   MATHILDE *nibbles the end of a slice of pizza.*

BIBI. Happiness has nothing to do with it.

STEPHEN. But a promotion has?

BIBI. I'm cooked. (*Points to herself.*) Malaria twice in eighteen months? Congo finally spat and shat me out.

   BIBI *takes a bite of pizza.*

SADHBH. I give you six months on East 42nd Street.

   SADHBH *takes a bite of pizza.*

STEPHEN. Why not *give her* / a break?

BIBI. I even sold the house in Kinshasa to – and you'll love this –
   To a Sister Addolorata. Big fat Italian nun with a cello.

STEPHEN. Because orphans just love Elgar.

BIBI. I think Bach is her thing but you got it.
   Yep – it's serious.
   I've shipped fifteen years of African knick-knacks to New York.
   My mom is nearly eighty – alone – in Philly.
   It's time I stopped running.
   I'm thirty-seven, baby! I wanna go home.

MATHILDE. I'm not running.

STEPHEN. Liar.

SADHBH. Don't mind him.

STEPHEN (*to* SADHBH). Just give me / a bit of pepperoni.

MATHILDE. I only want to do work I'm passionate about.

STEPHEN. Yeah, yeah. That's where we all started.
(*To* SADHBH.) Not pizza. The meat.

SADHBH *picks off some pepperoni bits and passes them to him*.

BIBI. That's pig's butt, you know.

STEPHEN. Fucking vegetarians. Pork butt is not pig butt –
She's trying to say I'm eating pig's asshole.

MATHILDE. What?

STEPHEN. We ate worse shit in Congo.

SADHBH. It's why she's vegetarian.

STEPHEN (*to* MATHILDE). Have you been to the DRC?

He eats.

MATHILDE. This will be my first time.

STEPHEN. What's your background?

MATHILDE. I've got a degree in Social Science, a Masters in
Humanitarian Assistance. And then of course internships at
ACF, Amnesty – Human Rights Watch –

STEPHEN. But not field work per se?

MATHILDE. No.

STEPHEN. How on earth did you get the job without
experience?

SADHBH. Stephen – you twat.

BIBI *picks up another slice of pizza*.

STEPHEN. I'll phrase it differently. Who did you sleep with?

MATHILDE. Maybe they realise you need education to learn from experience.

BIBI (*with her mouth full*). Can't tell you how many times I've saved his 'experienced' / sorry ass.

STEPHEN *laughs*.

STEPHEN. She's rewriting / history, Mathilde.

MATHILDE. I'm clear what I'm letting myself in for.

BIBI. Good, 'cause I've seen a lot of young people break down after only a few weeks in Congo – 'Oh, all the suffering.'

SADHBH. You get a cook, a cleaner, a driver and you get paid I'll be watching out for you.

BIBI. Your compound is fifteen kilometres from the displaced persons' camp in Masisi. It also houses MSF and Save the Children. Don't sleep with the doctors.
They never return your calls – and that's kind of awkward if you actually get sick.

MATHILDE. Okay.

BIBI. Your contact at the camp is Mama Carolina
– an experienced local health worker specialising in gender-based violence –
speaks about eight different languages.
She alerted us to the March massacres in Masisi.
She says a name keeps coming up – a Tutsi warlord called Colonel Jerome Mburame.
Any questions so far?

MATHILDE. We've postponed our trip twice because of violence. How is it now?

BIBI. It's been quiet in the area for over a month.
But be sensible. You and Sadhbh are in this together like a lifeboat.
One person's action or inaction will affect the other in terms of security.

MATHILDE. Of course. I understand.

STEPHEN. And if you don't like it you can always leave.

MATHILDE. I won't do that.

STEPHEN. I began as an idealist.
    I imagined I'd solve problems by day and at night I'd play
    guitar / under an African moon.

MATHILDE. What's wrong with idealism?

SADHBH. Stephen –

STEPHEN. We too – thought we could fix the world.
    We'd catapult ourselves in without a clue.

MATHILDE. I've done my homework.

STEPHEN. Good, because there's too much that's ineffective /
    about the work.

SADHBH. And he's off.

BIBI. I take issue with that, Stephen.

SADHBH. We all do.

BIBI. I've seen enormously successful programmes / in
    Congo –

STEPHEN. Really? And have they helped the Congolese
    become responsible for their own security? Have they fuck!

    MATHILDE *puts down her pizza and cleans her hands.*

    BIBI *and* SADHBH *look at one another. An awkward pause.*

MATHILDE. So you guys worked all together?

SADHBH. We met in –

STEPHEN. / 1999.

SADHBH. 2000 –

BIBI. 2000.

STEPHEN. Last time we all worked together / was in 2006.

BIBI. Worked, ate, had dysentery together.
I knew Sadhbh when she was running from a boy.
I'm not talking / about Stephen.

STEPHEN. Which boy?

SADHBH finishes her pizza and cleans her hands on some kitchen roll.

SADHBH. Oh – a sweetheart from home.
It was expected I'd end up / with him.
Does anyone want more pizza?

BIBI. The sweetheart was so pissed with you.

STEPHEN. I'll take that half-piece.

MATHILDE attempts to open another bottle of wine. The cork is stiff.

STEPHEN cleans his hands on kitchen roll.

SADHBH. Michael didn't understand. My parents didn't understand.

SADHBH gives STEPHEN a small slice.

I gave up a job in the bank to go to Congo with Oxfam. In Ireland that's like giving up the priesthood.

STEPHEN. Here – will I open / that for you?

MATHILDE. No, no. / It's okay – if I just – oh no.

The light flickers overhead. The light fades then blinks out.

The sound of tropical outdoors.

A spot of light. A CHILD in a grotty oversize football shirt is holding a rifle.

CHILD SOLDIER. *Descende de la voiture.*

STEPHEN steps into the light.

The CHILD gestures towards SADHBH and BIBI. They come forward.

The CHILD *gestures with the rifle that they should stop and raise their arms.*

STEPHEN. *Où est ton commandant?*

CHILD SOLDIER. *C'est moi. C'est moi le chef.*

STEPHEN. *Laisse-nous passer.*

CHILD SOLDIER. *Personne ne peut passer.*

SADHBH. *Nous avons nos papiers. Qui est ton commandant?*

BIBI. *Il ne sera pas content si tu ne nous laisses pas passer.*

CHILD SOLDIER. *Personne ne peut passer!*

STEPHEN. Hey, little buddy. Can you put down – ?

The CHILD *points the gun at* STEPHEN*'s head.*

(*Through gritted teeth.*) Fuck this shit.

SADHBH. Cool it. It's okay.

STEPHEN. Does this look okay to you?

CHILD SOLDIER. *Qu'est ce que t'as pour moi?*

STEPHEN. Just give her some dollars and let's go.

BIBI. What about chewing gum?

STEPHEN. You're kidding me, right?

SADHBH. Try to be calm.

CHILD SOLDIER *pokes the gun at* STEPHEN.

CHILD SOLDIER. Luyindula. Luyindula.

BIBI. What's she saying – ?

SADHBH. *Comment?*

BIBI. It's okay, Stephen, / it's okay.

STEPHEN (*through gritted teeth*). Good.
Because I'd rather not get shot in the face by an eight-year-old.

CHILD SOLDIER. Makélélé. Makélélé.

STEPHEN. Drogba.

CHILD SOLDIER. Drogba-Chelsea.

STEPHEN. Well done, little Buddy.

CHILD SOLDIER. LuaLua.

STEPHEN. You got me there, kiddo –

The CHILD SOLDIER *lifts the gun threateningly.*

CHILD SOLDIER. LuaLua.

She prepares to fire.

STEPHEN. Hang on... He's Newcastle – right?

CHILD SOLDIER. Newcastle United.

The CHILD *smiles at* STEPHEN.

Donne-moi.

STEPHEN *takes off his T-shirt and gives it to the* CHILD.
The CHILD *is delighted.*

(*Pointing to a logo on the T-shirt.*) *C'est quoi ca?*

STEPHEN. Adidas.

CHILD SOLDIER. A*dida. Adi das. J'aime Adi das.
Drogba, Makélélé, LuaLua.*

STEPHEN. LuaLua.

The light snaps out.

STEPHEN *is T-shirtless – holding his wine-stained top.*

SADHBH *throws* STEPHEN *a T-shirt.*

BIBI *clears up a pool of red wine with kitchen roll.*

MATHILDE. I'm so sorry.

STEPHEN. No worries. I love it when women / throw drink at
me.

MATHILDE. I'm a little drunk. Wow – (*Giggles*.) I didn't throw it.
You're funny.

SADHBH. You're hilarious.

STEPHEN *dabs at a spot of wine on* MATHILDE'*s knee and hands her the roll.*

MATHILDE *dabs at the spot of wine.*

MATHILDE. So – why did you leave Congo?

STEPHEN *picks up an empty bottle and some of the used kitchen roll.*

STEPHEN. I had a problem.

He clears the stuff away.

SADHBH. You didn't.

Stops him by handing him an empty tray with the remainders of pizza crusts.

STEPHEN. See, Mathilde – it's taboo for a humanitarian to say that they lost the plot.

SADHBH. What?

STEPHEN. Here's a bedtime story for you.
I finish a three-month contract in Congo. Sadhbh stays on. I arrive home. Back to normal. Pay the bills. Shopping in Sainsbury's. (*Dumps the rubbish into the bin and returns.*) Find myself standing at the fridge section for an hour in front of fifty kinds of yogurt – I've just come from a country without a fridge or fresh milk and don't let's even start on the meat counter. And this night – I'm woken by someone sitting on my bed. I realise that the bedroom is full of men, women, children. Some with splintered skulls.

MATHILDE. What did you do?

STEPHEN. I couldn't get out. The room being full.
So I have to pull the door. Really hard.
Maybe I even hurt people. Go for a piss – come back –

the fuckers are still there.
I can barely get back into the bed.

MATHILDE. And then?

STEPHEN. I discover that if I blink people disappear –
But only two or three per blink.
After a month I had a fully blown tic.

MATHILDE. But you're not blinking now?

STEPHEN. I went to see a shrink. Got some pills. Left my job.
Haven't looked back.

MATHILDE. You're joking with me?

STEPHEN. No. Yes. No.

MATHILDE. Oh dear, I must be drunk.
Silly. Silly. I can't tell it what you say is real.

The next-door neighbours resume hostilities.

STEPHEN. It was real.

BIBI *notes the disturbance.*

BIBI. And I thought this was a nice neighbourhood.

SADHBH. So did I.

STEPHEN *and* MATHILDE *smile at one another.* SADHBH
is irritated.

Can't we turn on / some music?

SADHBH *pours wine for* BIBI. STEPHEN *puts on some
music.*

MATHILDE. We go to Congo on Monday – you've welcomed
me.
Warned me. Thank you.

SADHBH. *Tu es ici chez toi.*

BIBI. I feel enormously reassured to hand over.

STEPHEN. She's the best.

SADHBH. Oh, come here.

She gives BIBI *a hug.*

STEPHEN *tops up* MATHILDE*'s wine glass.*

STEPHEN. Everyone looks for something in Congo.

MATHILDE. What?

STEPHEN. I hope you find it.
I didn't.

SADHBH *raises her glass.*

Mathilde's adventures.

They drink.

SADHBH. Bibi in New York.

BIBI. Home sweet home. I'll drink to that.

They drink.

And to Sadhbh and Stephen.
Together you still –
glow.

They drink. STEPHEN *and* SADHBH *look at one another.*

MATHILDE. *L'amour.* I'll drink to that.

They drink.

The music is turned up. STEPHEN *leans and kisses*
SADHBH.

I want to remember this.

Music. The row echoes through the music.

Three

North Kivu.

Democratic Republic of Congo.

MATHILDE *steps outside the compound.* (*A gated area, which houses a number of NGOs.*)

A WOMAN *in a bright headscarf carrying a sick baby accosts* MATHILDE.

She is speaking Swahili – and very fast. They speak across one another.

WOMAN. *Dada, dada, tafazali, Unisaidie. Mume wange ni mugunjwa sana na motto wangu naye pia. / Sijuwe nifanye nini. Ninakuomba, dada!* [Madame? Madame, please? You must help me. My husband is very sick and now my baby is sick. I don't know what to do. Please help me.]

MATHILDE. *Tu parles français?*

WOMAN. *Tafadhali, Tafadhali Saidia uyu / binti wangu.* [Please. Please. Save my little girl.]

MATHILDE. *Je comprends pas.*
Francais? English?

WOMAN. *Dawa kwa binti wangu? Dakitari, dakitari?* [Medicine for my daughter. Doctor. Doctor?]

MATHILDE. *Pardon, je comprends pas.*

WOMAN. *Dawa, dawa! Medico? / Medico?* [Medicine. Medicine?]

MATHILDE. *Medico? Je suis pas medécin!* [Medico? I'm not a doctor.]

WOMAN. *Tafadhali. Nisaidie. Dola, / dola.* [Dollars. Dollars. Please help me.]

MATHILDE. *Dola? Tu veux dire dollars?*
J'ai pas de dollars sur moi, mais.

WOMAN. *Unaweza kunipeleka kwa dakitari? Mtoto wangu*
apa hatari ya kufa. Anaitiji matibabu. / Dada anaitaji Dawa:
Kwa nini huwezi nisaidia? [Can you take me to a doctor?
My daughter is dying. She needs medicine lady. Why will
you not help me?]

MATHILDE. *Pardon. Je comprends pas, mais si tu viens avec*
moi. On pourra trouver quelqu'un qui parle Swahili. Juste la
au portail. / Médecins? La? MSF. Tu comprends?

WOMAN. *Kamata motto wangu. Hakuna namna ingine*
ninaweza mufanya. Umusaidie. / Umupe maisha mema.
[Take my baby. You must take her. There is nothing I can do
for her. You can save her.]

MATHILDE. *Peux-tu venir avec moi? Viens avec moi.*

The WOMAN *pushes the baby into* MATHILDE*'s arms.*

Non. Non. Toi tu tiens ton enfant: moi – je vais chercher de
l'aide.

MATHILDE *tries to give the* WOMAN *her baby back but*
the WOMAN *steps away.*

WOMAN. *Hapana. Hapana shika / mtoto wangu. Msaidie.*
[No. no. You must take my baby. Make her better.]

MATHILDE. *Oh mon Dieu. Ton bébé tremble. Ca fait combien*
de temps qu'elle est? Oh mon Dieu!

WOMAN. *Mungu atakusaidia. Msaidie. Ni motto mzuri sana.*
Hakuna kitu niwezacho fanya. [Bless you. Be kind to her.
She is a very good daughter. There is nothing more I can do.]

The WOMAN *moves away.*

MATHILDE. Hey! *Tu vas où? Reviens!*

The WOMAN *runs away.*

Hey! Come back!

MATHILDE *looks at the baby.*

Petite princesse.

MATHILDE *listens to her heart.*

Ah non! Mon Dieu.

She tries to resuscitate the baby. She fails.

She takes out her VHF handheld radio.

Sierra Kilo. Sierra Kilo. This is Mike Romeo over.

SADHBH. This is Sierra Kilo. Mike Romeo send.

MATHILDE. I'm outside the compound. There's a sick baby. She's dying. I need help.

SADHBH. Hang in there. We're moving. Over.

MATHILDE. I think it might be too late.

SADHBH. We'll be right there. We'll be right there.

MATHILDE *listens to the baby's heart. The baby is dead.*

MATHILDE. *Oh, non. Non!*

MATHILDE *closes the baby's eyes and whispers in her ear.*

Chut, chut, chut. Là, là! Chut, chut.

She stops. SADHBH *runs on.*

She's dead. I'm sorry.

SADHBH. It's okay.

SADHBH *tries to take the baby from* MATHILDE.

MATHILDE. I'm sorry.

SADHBH. Give me the baby, Mathilde.

SADHBH *takes the baby from* MATHILDE *and helps her to stand.*

MATHILDE. I'm sorry, I'm sorry.

SADHBH. It's okay. It's okay.

They exit.

Four

Night. A tropical night. A shot in the far distance.

The compound.

SADHBH *is sitting on a wooden crate working on her laptop. She's sipping a glass of whiskey.* MATHILDE *approaches her.*

MATHILDE. Emailing Stephen?

SADHBH. When I'm here I want to be there and when I'm there I want to be here.

MATHILDE. You did not eat this evening.

> SADHBH *shrugs.*

> But you drink whiskey?

SADHBH. I can always drink whiskey.

> SADHBH *passes her a bottle and a glass.*

> I was expecting you.
> You okay?

> MATHILDE *shrugs. She pours a drink and drinks it back.*

> Atta girl.

> MATHILDE *pours another and sits beside* SADHBH.

> You shouldn't have left the compound today.

MATHILDE. So we gate ourselves in here?

SADHBH. Yeah. We do.

MATHILDE. And we travel to the camps –
They're crowded – they're awful.
We listen to the stories and then we come back to our nice compound again.

SADHBH. And we don't go out the gate.
    Not by yourself anyway.

    MATHILDE *takes a sip of whiskey.*

MATHILDE. I thought I heard a gunshot.

SADHBH. When?

MATHILDE. Oh God. It *was* a gunshot.

SADHBH. There's been a pocket of fighting about thirty
    kilometres away but MONUC have reassured me that it's
    minor.

MATHILDE. Why didn't you tell me?

SADHBH. What's the point in worrying you?
    I didn't want to worry you.

MATHILDE. Well, I'm worried now.

SADHBH. Don't be.
    We have Janvier – our security. He's totally on the ball.
    Any sign of trouble in this area – we're gone.
    I'm not putting anybody's life at risk – including my own.

    MATHILDE *gets up and walks away.*

    We're not in Kansas now.

    MATHILDE *flashes* SADHBH *a look.*

MATHILDE. My father passed away when I was eight. It made
    me very aware of life and death. I thought – this work – I
    could help others.
    What a stupid fucked idea that was.

SADHBH. You've been here less than a month. Don't be so
    hard on yourself.

MATHILDE. Yes. What do I expect but –
    *Je crois – Je veux croire qu'il puisse y avoir justice pour tout
    ces gens –*
    Maybe I can do nothing but bear witness. But do I change
    anything? / What am I doing? Tell me.

SADHBH. If you wanted to be an instant lifesaver you should
have worked for MSF.

MATHILDE. Okay.

SADHBH. Even so – you probably couldn't have saved the
baby's life today.

MATHILDE. No. No. I can't think about that.

SADHBH. Mathilde – we believe in justice –
   but it takes time –
   so –
   We write the reports.
   Each testimony helps identify the perpetrator.
   And someday – it might change things.
   Listen –
   If you don't want to travel to the camp tomorrow I /
   absolutely understand.

MATHILDE. Don't try to protect me, Sadhbh. This does not
   work for me. If there is gunfire don't tell me it is
   firecrackers.
   Don't tell me not to go out the fucking gate because I will
   anyway. Don't treat me like a stupid kid.
   It will be a privilege to hear the stories tomorrow.
   I want to be there.

   SADHBH *pours herself another drink. She looks at*
   MATHILDE.

   MATHILDE *looks away.*

SADHBH. We've got R and R coming up.
   We'll go to Goma.
   Let off steam. It works for me anyway.

MATHILDE. Sounds good.

   A gunshot in the far distance.

   MATHILDE *freezes.*

   What was that?

SADHBH. You heard it as well as I did.

SADHBH *picks up her things and goes indoors.*

MATHILDE *tries to brave it for a moment and then runs.*

Five

A makeshift hut in an IDP camp.

A dirt floor. SADHBH *and* MATHILDE *are sitting together.*

SADHBH *takes up her writing materials. Throughout the scene she writes down* AMALA*'s testimony.* AMALA *is with* MAMA CAROLINA

MATHILDE *simultaneously translates.*

SADHBH. Mama Carolina says you want to tell your story. Is that right, Amala?

MATHILDE. *Mama Carolina dit que tu voudrais raconter ton histoire, Amala? C'est vrai?*

AMALA *nods.*

MAMA CAROLINA. *Prends ton temps.*

AMALA *leans in to whisper to* MAMA CAROLINA.

She wants to know if you will write all of this in your book?

SADHBH. I will. Is that okay, Amala?

MAMA CAROLINA. *Tu es d'accord?*

AMALA *nods. She leans into* MAMA CAROLINA *who speaks for her.*

Thunder killed my mother.

SADHBH. Thunder?

MAMA CAROLINA (*sotto voce*). Grenade.
  The Tutsi rebels – Banyamulenge – they took my brother.

MATHILDE. *Est-ce qu'ils portaient un uniforme?*

  AMALA *nods*.

MAMA CAROLINA. They are wearing a uniform—with a
  yellow band around the arm.
  The rebels fire fire all the houses in the village.

SADHBH. Amala – What happened next?

MATHILDE. *Qu'est ce qui s'est passé ensuite?*

MAMA CAROLINA. The thunder is coming – louder – louder.
  Me and my mama we run, run, run.
  She falls – the thunder comes.
  I run but the soldiers catch me.
  They say 'your mother is dead. We are your new family'.

SADHBH. Where did the soldiers take you?

MATHILDE. *Où t'ont emmenée les soldats.*

MAMA CAROLINA. We walk a long time. There is a camp.
  They took me to the Commandant and he says, 'You are my
  wife now.'

SADHBH. What is the Commandant's name?

MATHILDE. *Comment s'appelle le Commandant?*

MAMA CAROLINA. Everybody knows his name.
  Commandant Jerome Mburame.
  I am his wife so I cook for him and clean his shoes. He likes
  his shoes very nice.
  And I sleep with him so he is happy.

SADHBH. And Amala, are you happy with Commandant
  Jerome?

MATHILDE. *Est ce que toi tu étais heureuse?*

  AMALA *shakes her head*.

MAMA CAROLINA. He frightens me. I can't always make
him happy.
I try to escape – but the soldiers catch me and then the
Commandant says he doesn't want me for his wife any more
so the soldiers take me to the forest and tie me to a tree.

SADHBH. *Ça va, Amala?*

MAMA CAROLINA. It was better when I was the wife.

SADHBH. Amala, did the soldiers hurt you?

MATHILDE. *Ils t'ont fait mal?*

> AMALA *nods. She leans into* MAMA CAROLINA.

MAMA CAROLINA. Night and day. Day and night.
They say, 'Your village is destroyed. Your mother is dead.
And soon you will be dead.'

SADHBH. Can you tell me how many soldiers hurt you,
Amala?

MATHILDE. *Combien de soldats t'ont fait mal?*

MAMA CAROLINA. I think – twelve.
They say I belong to the Interhamwe.
I say I belong to my maman.

MATHILDE. *Tu te souviens de leurs noms?*

MAMA CAROLINA. The leader. They call him Sergeant.
He laughs when he hurts me.
I shout and shout and he says
'No one can hear you.
No one is listening.'
One day they forget me. They do not come back and I run,
run, run, I walk, walk, walk.

SADHBH. And Mama Carolina found you?

> AMALA *nods.*

MAMA CAROLINA. She thinks I'm a ghost because I'm
covered in white dust. I do not know if I am alive or if I am
dead.

Mama Carolina – she brings me to this camp.
She says 'Amala. You are alive.'

AMALA *steps away from* MAMA CAROLINA *and speaks for herself.*

AMALA. *Je peux venir habiter avec toi. Je serais sage.*

MAMA CAROLINA. *Calme – toi, ma petite Amala.*

AMALA. *J'ai tellement peur de rester ici.*

MAMA CAROLINA. *T'inquiete pas, Amala. Viens ici.*

SADHBH. If I take you home then I have to take everyone home and I can't do that.

AMALA. *Ici je pleure tout le temps.*

AMALA *throws herself into* SADHBH's *arms.*

Tu peux être ma maman. Mama Sadhbh. Mama Sadhbh.

SADHBH *comforts* AMALA.

MAMA CAROLINA. *T'inquiete pas, Amala. Viens ici.*

MAMA CAROLINA *extracts* AMALA *from* SADHBH's *arms.*

C'est l'heure de dejeuner.

AMALA. *Ton chapeau?*

Je l'aime bien. Tu es blanche.

SADHBH *hands her the hat.*

SADHBH. The sun makes me – (*Mimes a burnt face.*) rouge!

AMALA *giggles and puts on the hat.*

Amala. We want to stop Colonel Jerome and his soldiers hurting people.

MATHILDE. *Nous voulons l'empêcher de continuer á faire du mal.*

AMALA. *Tu dois le tuer!*

MATHILDE. *C'est le juge qui va décider.*

AMALA *leans into* MAMA CAROLINA.

MAMA CAROLINA. Will he be there?

MATHILDE. *Non. Ca sera en huis clos.*

SADHBH. You will tell your story to the judge. You won't see the Colonel.

AMALA. *Si tu es là, Mama, je peux raconter mon histoire.*

MAMA CAROLINA. *Amala, tu es courageuse.*

SADHBH. Then I will be there. I will be there.

Six

A bumpy and noisy clattering car journey.

The compound.

SADHBH *is leaning against a wall.*

SADHBH. Oh, man.

MATHILDE. You are unwell again? Hey, don't faint. Ai ai.

    MATHILDE *drags over a crate and makes* SADHBH *sit on it.*

Put your head between your legs.

SADHBH *does so.* MATHILDE *crouches beside her.*

That is a hell of a drive.
Sometimes I'm thinking are we gonna make it?

MATHILDE *takes* SADHBH*'s hand.*

Better?

SADHBH *nods.*

SADHBH. A country without roads.
    Hard to imagine until you are actually here.

MATHILDE. I can no longer feel my backside.

    SADHBH *laughs*. MATHILDE *rubs* SADHBH*'s back*.

    Today was too much, ah? The heat too.
    You want to lie down in your room?

    MATHILDE *takes a bottle of water from her bag*.

SADHBH. No, no no.

    She hands it to SADHBH *who drinks*.

MATHILDE. You want the whiskey in it?

    SADHBH *shakes her head*.

SADHBH. I draw the line at afternoon drinking.

    SADHBH *holds out her hand to* MATHILDE.

    You did well today. Thank you.

MATHILDE. Ahh – all the stories are mushed in my head.
    I don't know… very shocking.

    She breathes out.

    The little girl we first interviewed today.
    Amala – Oh my heart. It hurts.

SADHBH. There's always one like Amala – who catches your
    eye –

    The sound of a gate being banged.

MATHILDE. She was Mburame's 'wife'.
    This is important testimony. *Non?*

SADHBH. I made her a promise I shouldn't have.
    I don't know where I'll be if it ever goes to trial.

    The sound of a gate being banged.

MATHILDE. What do you mean 'ever'?
    The evidence against Mburame and his troops stacks up? We
    talked to twenty / women today who –

SADHBH. Mathilde – We're a human rights organisation – not the police, the army or the government. Our work puts pressure on other players to act. So we must present them fucking good evidence!

MATHILDE. So – we write up the report now, now, now. Let's call for his arrest.

SADHBH. None of those twenty women agreed to testify. Do you understand?

MATHILDE. I didn't think –

SADHBH. This is just the beginning.

A FEMALE SOLDIER *in army fatigues enters holding an AK-47.*

SOLDIER. Madame Sadhbh!

SADHBH. That's me.

SOLDIER. *Toi, viens avec moi!*

SADHBH. No. I don't think so.

SOLDIER. *J'ai reçu des instructions.*

SADHBH. From who?

The SOLDIER *hands over a letter.*

SADHBH *reads the letter.*

MATHILDE. What is going on?

SOLDIER. *J'ai reçu des instructions.*

SADHBH. Put away your gun.

SOLDIER. *Okay, madame. Pardon.*

The SOLDIER *slings the gun across her back.*

SADHBH. You have frightened us.

SOLDIER. *Excuse-moi si je t'ai effrayé.*

SADHBH. Why did you do that?

SADHBH *hands* MATHILDE *the letter.*

SOLDIER. *Pardon, madame.*
Tu peux enmener ton garde du corps. / S'il te plait, ne le dit pas au commandant: il sera fâché contre moi.

MATHILDE. You're not thinking of going?

SADHBH. Of course not.

SOLDIER. Madame. Please. Please.
Je ne peux pas retourner sans vous.

SADHBH. Don't go back. You don't have to.

SOLDIER. *Alors là vous m'avez tuée!*

MATHILDE. / She says you have killed her.

SADHBH. Oh – crap.

MATHILDE. Can we help? What / can we –

SADHBH. My security guard and I will travel in our own car.

MATHILDE. What?

SOLDIER. *Bien sur, madame.* You will follow me.

SADHBH. Okay. Wait outside, please.

SOLDIER. *Pardon, madame. Pardon.*

The SOLDIER *slopes off.*

MATHILDE. So – I'm coming with you. Let's go.

SADHBH. Janvier will be with me.

MATHILDE. But it's crazy.

SADHBH. I've been meeting with warlords for years.

MATHILDE. What does that mean?

SADHBH. I'm going without you.

MATHILDE. No. No. No. I am very unhappy about this.

SADHBH. I'm looking forward to the chat.

She turns and MATHILDE *physically stops her.*

MATHILDE. Stop. Just stop.
   You are trembling.

SADHBH. Let me go. If we're not back in two hours call
   MONUC.

SADHBH *exits.*

MATHILDE *calls after her.*

MATHILDE. Hey! We're in this together like a lifeboat?

Seven

Makeshift military headquarters.

SADHBH *is waiting. She is sitting by a small table and has a
book and pen.*

COLONEL MBURAME *enters. He is dressed in army fatigues.
He wears a black beret and has a yellow band on his shoulder.
He is wearing army boots polished to a high shine.*

SADHBH *stands.*

SADHBH. *Bonjour.*
   Merci pour votre invitation.

   COLONEL MBURAME *beckons for her to sit down.*

COLONEL MBURAME. *Je vous en prie.*

SADHBH. *Colonel Mburame, vous êtes la première personne
   que je voulais venir saluer. / Est-ce que on peut parler?*

COLONEL MBURAME. Why do you not wear a wedding
   ring? Madame?

SADHBH. Kavanagh. Are you aware who I work for?

COLONEL MBURAME. Of course.

SADHBH. DDH is a neutral organisation. We are not linked / to any government.

COLONEL MBURAME. You are not married, Madame Kavanagh?

SADHBH. I was hoping we could –

The FEMALE SOLDIER *returns with a tray carrying two teacups and a pot of tea.*

COLONEL MBURAME. English breakfast?

SADHBH. Thank you.

The FEMALE SOLDIER *pours the tea.*

COLONEL MBURAME. Rumour has it you sleep with all the men. But we understand about radio of the pavement in this country.

He looks to the FEMALE SOLDIER. *She smiles and nods.*

SADHBH. I was hoping we could talk about the situation in Masisi.

COLONEL MBURAME. Are you a politician?

SADHBH. Now that we have this opportunity I was –

The FEMALE SOLDIER *gives* SADHBH *a cup of tea.*

COLONEL MBURAME. You have answered none of my questions – but I must answer yours?

SADHBH. Go ahead.

The FEMALE SOLDIER *gives* COLONEL MBURAME *a cup of tea.*

COLONEL MBURAME. Where are you from?

SADHBH. Ireland.

COLONEL MBURAME. Top of the morning to you.

SADHBH. Very good.

COLONEL MBURAME. I was taught by a Sister Bernadette from Tipperary. Do you know this place?

SADHBH. Yes. I do.

COLONEL MBURAME. She made us sing hymns all the days.

'*Venez donc, les petits enfants, chantons tous ensemble –
parce que Jesus vous aime chaque jour.*'

COLONEL MBURAME *smiles. He laughs. He encourages
the* FEMALE SOLDIER *to laugh.*

Sister Bernadette was a farmer's daughter.
Are you one such?

SADHBH. No. But I grew up surrounded by farmland.
I can milk a cow.

COLONEL MBURAME. Myself? – I was brought up on a
farm. I too can milk a cow,
Tell me why are you going around asking questions?

SADHBH. Colonel Mburame. I've heard a very concerning
issue that I'd like to raise with you.

COLONEL MBURAME *dismisses the* FEMALE SOLDIER
with a wave. The FEMALE SOLDIER *steps back and stands
to attention – her AK-47 slung in front of her body.*

I've spoken at length with individuals and this is what I
understand happened.
Your troops attacked the town of Masisi.

COLONEL MBURAME. *C'est faux.*

SADHBH. Over thirty people were murdered. Many were
tortured and mutilated.

COLONEL MBURAME. Hyper *faux.*

SADHBH. On March 4th your troops raped fifty-three women.
Colonel. I'd be very interested to hear your reaction to that.

COLONEL MBURAME. Madame Kavanagh. I am not a
warlord.
I am a protector of my people.

SADHBH. Colonel Mburame – again these are allegations – but
I also heard that your soldiers went to the St Thérese School

– picked out girls and raped them, held them prisoner over a period of three weeks and then left them in the road. / Seven young women have told me that and I understand there are more.

COLONEL MBURAME. I can't believe this.

SADHBH. I've heard allegations that girls as young as eight years old were brought to you and made sex slaves for you and your soldiers.

COLONEL MBURAME. *Comment osez-vous dire ca?* Are you not ashamed to accuse me of this?

SADHBH. There are people who specifically identify your troops in the attack. There are people who identify you.

COLONEL MBURAME. Has the genocide taught you nothing about Hutu liars and killers?

SADHBH. The type of uniform your group wears was identified.

COLONEL MBURAME. This is what you base your claims upon?
You realise these uniforms can be bought.
Our enemies are known to have done this before. *C'est faux, faux, arche faux.*

SADHBH. Why are so many people talking about it? You –
Colonel Mburame will be held accountable for the actions of your men.
Are you aware that these kind of crimes are war crimes?

COLONEL MBURAME. Maybe a few of my soldiers on this occasion got a bit crazy. You know what it's like –
They just had a bit too much to drink but in my armed group we're very serious about that. I will make sure I find the perpetrators of these acts and they will be shot.
Dites moi qui a dit ça?
Tell me the names of the victims so I can go and talk to them directly.

SADHBH. Why would I give you their names?
Would you mind not pointing your gun at me?

COLONEL MBURAME. *Vous ne pouvez pas comprendre,*
comment pouvez-vous comprendre?

SADHBH. Colonel Mburame.

COLONEL MBURAME. *J'essaie de protéger mon peuple.*
Whatever I have to do to protect my people is whatever I
have to do.
Comment s'appellent ils? Montrez les moi!

   COLONEL MBURAME *grabs her notebook. He flicks*
   quickly through it.

SADHBH. There are no names. It's a list of the allegations.

   He reads through them.

COLONEL MBURAME. Why is this the business of the Irish?

SADHBH. My business here concerns serious violations of
international humanitarian and human rights law.

COLONEL MBURAME. The white angel from the west –
Come to drag me to The Hague!
Is this not so?

SADHBH. I believe that things can be better, Colonel
Mburame.

COLONEL MBURAME. Drink your tea, Madame Kavanagh.

   She does as she is told.

   He hands back the book.

   Write – 'It was never meant to happen this way.'

SADHBH. What wasn't?

COLONEL MBURAME. Some people were killed but that
wasn't my fault.
Je ne suis pas coupable.
Write that in your book.

SADHBH. I will.

COLONEL MBURAME. Write – 'It wasn't these two hands.'
Ce n'était pas ces mains,

ce n'était pas ces mains.
Tell that to your relevant authorities. Go home, Madame
Kavanagh.
This is not your business. This is not your war.

COLONEL MBURAME *stands.*

When I was a child there were massacres in my village. The
blue helmets stood by as my father's cattle were stolen, his
farm burned to the ground.
My mother murdered with a hammer.
The Hutu killers did not want to waste a bullet and cutting is
such hard work. You are looking at my cut.
Touch me. Touch me. (*Grabs her hand and presses it on his
forehead.*) A survivor's scar.
The wound festered with squirming insects for three weeks. I
was left for dead, Madame Kavanagh.

He releases her hand.

This is your international concern?
Your 'humanitarian assistance'?
We want none of it.
My conscience is clear.

COLONEL MBURAME *drinks his tea. He puts down his
cup.*

Pause.

And now, Madame Kavanagh, I fear I must leave you.

SADHBH *stands up.*

Non! Attendez ici. I'll tell your driver to come here. It's
getting dark. *C'est plus prudent de rester ici jusqu'à
l'arrivée de votre escorte.*

SADHBH. Thank you, Colonel Mburame. I will think carefully
about what you have said. I hope you do likewise.

COLONEL MBURAME *exits.* SADHBH *sits. She looks at
the* FEMALE SOLDIER. *The* FEMALE SOLDIER *looks
straight ahead.*

End of Act One.

ACT TWO

One

Goma. A house party.

A noisy party scene – with Congolese Soukous music – dim lighting – perhaps candles – oil lamps. There are bottles, bodies, snogging, red plastic chairs, a string of lights, perhaps a poster advertising Primus.

People are dancing. There is an atmosphere of abandon.

After some moments the other bodies move on and RONAN and VIN are revealed. They are drinking bottles of Primus. The party still ongoing but at a much lower level.

RONAN (*an Irish Foreign correspondent*) *is talking with* VIN (*a young photographer*).

RONAN. You came to Goma on a punt?

VIN. Yeah. I think if I can get good pictures and a story.
    Maybe someone like the *Sunday Times* will buy my work.

RONAN. Who do you know at the *Sunday Times*?

VIN. My mum's cousin is married to the editor of the Travel section.

RONAN. Brilliant.

VIN. I've heard people talking about Masisi.
    You're going there, right?

RONAN. Right.

VIN. They say – it's violent. Murderous.
    It's a restaurant for flies. They feast.

RONAN. What twat said that?
    I wrote it, didn't I.

VIN. Yeah – but that's why I wanted to talk to you.
A girl from Médecins sans Frontières said you might be able
to help me.

RONAN. How?

VIN. You'll need a photographer, right?

RONAN. I have a photographer.

VIN. I could just watch you?

RONAN. No. How do you intend to get to Masisi?

VIN. I'll hire a motorbike.

RONAN *laughs*.

RONAN. I've never seen a roadworthy bike in Congo –
And the roads from Goma to Masisi / are terrible.

VIN. You can get stuck in mud. You can get held up. Robbed.
I know.

RONAN. I have security when I travel.
You know that too. Right?

VIN. If I'm prepared to come here then I'm prepared to take the
risks.

RONAN. Rule number one – the only rule –
No job is worth your life.
Why do you want to risk your life for an article –

VIN. Photo essay. I'm a / photographer.

RONAN. For a photo essay no one is going to want?
This is an ongoing story so unless you've got a commission?
Or find a story about cannibalism – maybe child-raping
peacekeepers…

VIN. Yeah. Okay.

RONAN. Man!
You need papers to go anywhere.

VIN. I have a letter from the *Walthamstow Guardian*.

RONAN. That'll be a great help.

VIN. Yeah, yeah. Okay.

RONAN. You can't just rock up to a village and take your
    camera out.

VIN. Will you help me or not?

RONAN. Forget it.
    It's a responsibility.

    VIN *takes a book out of his backpack*.

VIN. Have a look at my pictures.

RONAN. Why not.

    RONAN *flicks through the shots*.

VIN. Those are of the flood near Cockermouth – the collapse of
    Lorton Bridge. It was incredible – my dad is an RAF
    squadron leader and we –

RONAN. The good news is – you've got talent.

VIN. And the bad news?

RONAN. You haven't a fucking clue why you're good.

    There's nothing about this shot that tells me it's
    Cockermouth or anywhere for that matter. It's a wanky arty
    picture of water.

    He flicks through the other pictures.

    You've got to have purpose behind the image. Got it?
    And I don't give a shit who your dad is.

VIN. I learn quickly.

RONAN. That helps.

VIN. I've got passion and honesty.

RONAN. So did a lot of dead photographers.

    Hands him back his portfolio.

    The face is very powerful. Don't be afraid of the obvious.
    Not bad, though.

VIN. Brilliant. Thanks. Thanks so much.

RONAN. For nothing. It's just an opinion. Take it or leave it.

He hands VIN *back the portfolio.*

Man, your best bet is to bed one of the aid workers.

VIN. What?

RONAN. They've got security, the houses, the cars and the contacts.

VIN. Do you know someone I can talk to? Anybody here?

RONAN. Look around. What do you see?

VIN. Wall-to-wall women.

RONAN. If I were you I would go back to the nice girl from Médecins sans Frontières and ask to see her stamp collection.
They're not called 'Nurses Without Knickers' for nothing.

VIN. Really?

RONAN *rolls his eyes.*

VIN *scans the room for the sex-starved.* RONAN *writes something on a bit of paper.*

RONAN. Buddy?

VIN. Yes?

RONAN. This is not your playground. It's a dangerous place.

He hands him the piece of paper.

That's where I'm staying.
We're leaving at 6 a.m. and won't be waiting.

VIN. Are you serious?

RONAN. Jaysus, don't hug me. Get me a beer / for fuck's sake.

VIN. Excellent. Thank you. Bloody brilliant.
Will do.

VIN *wanders off and bumps smack into* SADHBH *and* MATHILDE.

RONAN (*to himself*). Ahh, Jesus wept.

VIN. Ladies! Can I get you a drink?

SADHBH. We're okay.

MATHILDE. It's okay.

RONAN. The Kincasslagh Kavanagh.
     How the hell are you?

SADHBH. Not too shabby.

RONAN. And who is this vision?

SADHBH. Pick on someone your own age.

MATHILDE. Mathilde Rolla

She holds out her hand and he shakes it.

Sadhbh's assistant.

RONAN. Ronan Fitzgerald.
     Sadhbh's admirer.

SADHBH. He's like this with everyone.

RONAN *pulls out a bottle of Jägermeister and shot glasses.*

It's going to be one of those nights, is it?

He pours three shots.

RONAN. Pull up a couple of pews there, Mathilde.

MATHILDE *drags over a chair.*

SADHBH. There's something very wrong about drinking Jägermeister in Africa.

RONAN. Gowanouttathat. Get up the yard.

He knocks back a shot.

They knock back a shot.

MATHILDE. It's gone 'up the yard' and tastes like medicine.

RONAN. Numbs the brain and warms the heart.
Just what the doctor ordered.

SADHBH. What's the craic?

RONAN. I've just been in Kigali covering Jean Butler's visit to
some genocide sites – Jean Butler's visit to some 'Maison
des Veuves'. Jean Butler visits gorillas in the fucking mist.

MATHILDE. Who is Jean Butler?

RONAN. Did the nineties completely pass you by?
Jean Butler – Riverdance – the Eurovision?

SADHBH. What's she doing in Kigali?

RONAN. Teaching Rwandans to Riverdance. I don't fucking
know, Sadhbh.

SADHBH. It's a PR visit.

RONAN. Lovely girl an' all – don't get me wrong – but there
must be a more edifying way to make a livin'.
And Kigali is a fuckin joke.
There are so many NGOs they're trippin' over one another
and they'll tell you the best place to get steak and where the
jazz clubs are but they haven't a fucking clue about the
disaster that's happening in North Kivu – I've been thinking
about running an article on it.
Lazy fat-arse NGOs driving around in their four-by-fours
while Masisi burns a couple of hours drive away.
Let's tell people exactly where their direct debit is going.

SADHBH. No aid agency will touch you with a shitty stick if
you run that story.

RONAN. It's time we had a grown-up debate about the C-word
in the aid world.

SADHBH. Corruption is a red herring, Ronan.
For God's sake – don't print stuff that will stop people
giving.

I mean – our organisation daren't mention that donations are spent on office chairs. But you know – we have an office.

He pours them another shot.

RONAN. Are you suggesting your organisation be impervious to scrutiny?

SADHBH. I'm saying – recognise the impact of negative sentiment.

RONAN. True enough.
Another poncey party full of bleeding-heart aid workers. Shouldn't you be in some hole lassoing warlords?

SADHBH. We've got R and R for a couple of days – Stephen is in Tanzania on business so we're going to try to – connect – if he can hitch a ride here.

RONAN *looks at* SADHBH *flirtatiously.*

RONAN. He was a locationship, wasn't he?

SADHBH. Yep. I met Stephen exactly same time I met you.

RONAN *looks away.*

RONAN. He got there just before I did.

SADHBH. 'We' were never on the cards.

RONAN. Oh yes we were. Don't think you can deny it.
Mathilde, this woman could have changed me.

SADHBH. I doubt that somehow.

RONAN. Is he missing you? The poor fucker.
Must be awful when the girlfriend is married to the job.
How do you keep it going? You here – him there.

SADHBH. We manage.

RONAN *takes a large draught of his beer.*

RONAN. Don't tell him I was asking for him.

SADHBH. I won't.

They clink glasses and drink a shot each.

RONAN. So what are you, Mathilde?

MATHILDE. Excuse me?

RONAN. Mercenary? Missionary? Misfit? All of the above?

MATHILDE. Who is this guy?

SADHBH. Don't pay any heed to him.

RONAN. That's all Congo needs.
Another mental female with a big heart.

VIN *delivers* RONAN*'s beer.*

Vin, meet Sadhbh Kavanagh – very senior human rights
researcher here in Congo. /
And her glamorous assistant Mathilde Rolla.
You should pick their brains on Masisi.

VIN. Hi. Hi.
Oh, really?

MATHILDE. We've just come from there.

RONAN. Whose party is this anyway?

SADHBH. Did you never meet Romy – big tall dark-haired girl
– / Doctor with the Red Cross?

MATHILDE (*to* VIN). We've just been investigating.

RONAN. She's Irish?

SADHBH. She's putting us / up for a few nights.

VIN (*to* MATHILDE). Sorry?

MATHILDE (*to* VIN). In Masisi. The attack on the Hutu –

RONAN. Dr Romy from Kinlough? Indeed. I know her
intimately.

SADHBH. Of course you do. /
Hit me again.

VIN (*to* MATHILDE). I'd love to talk to you about it.

RONAN *pours them another shot.*

The music flares up.

SADHBH. So what's next?

VIN. What's your NGO?

MATHILDE. What?

RONAN. I'm doing a feature for the *Irish Times*. / Travelling to Masisi tomorrow with a team from Concern.

MATHILDE (*to* VIN). Let's move outside.

SADHBH. I bump into them every day. / Any of them here?

He turns around to look.

RONAN. Maybe not. We have a / 6 a.m. start.

VIN (*to* MATHILDE). Great.

VIN *and* MATHILDE *move away from* RONAN *and* SADHBH.

RONAN. You've just come from Masisi?

SADHBH. A bad bad scene.
How long are you there for?

RONAN. If I get a story quick enough I may well be back in Dublin by Thursday. I want to get back to the wee fella.

SADHBH. Is your ex letting you see him now?

RONAN. After much legal wrangling.

He takes out his phone and shows her his screen saver.

There's Seanie.

SADHBH *looks at the picture.*

I've cleaned up my act, I'm not drinking as much. The *New York Times* picked up my last couple of articles.
Slowly but surely – it's a fucker, you know?
The wee fella is playing his first football match tomorrow and I'm not there.

SADHBH. So change job.

RONAN. Fuck that.

They knock back the shots.

Any stories for me?

SADHBH. I interviewed Colonel Jerome Mburame.

RONAN. Get the fuck out! How did you manage that?

SADHBH. He found me.

RONAN. Ahhh – squeezed you in between pillaging and
raping?
The dote.

SADHBH. His army boots are polished to a Sandhurst shine.
His English is superb.
Better than mine.

RONAN. And he's an out-and-out mad bollix.

SADHBH. He says he's protecting his people from a second
genocide.

RONAN. Amazing how he's managing to get rich on it.
Nothing to do with tin and tantalum mines then!
So, Miss Kavanagh. Hanging with Mr Warlord?
Madness and chaos. Living on the edge, baby.
You love all that.

SADHBH. I never stop loving it. This is true.
Nothing feels more right than to do the work.
You – on the other hand – are a jealous alcoholic hack.
You'd eat your arm off for a chat with Mburame.

RONAN. Only my mother knows me as well as you do.
Where is he?

SADHBH. Go fuck yourself.

RONAN *drinks a shot.*

RONAN. Funnily enough I was thinking isn't it about time we
had a ride?

SADHBH. Classy, Ronan. Classy. I *did* tell you Stephen was coming tomorrow?

RONAN. I'll be the warm-up act. You're a fine thing. I am not too appalling. And I bet you're in severe need of a ride.

SADHBH. Strangely – I'm not in severe need of a ride – but I tell you what I will do?

RONAN. What?

SADHBH. I'll get us a proper drink. Jägermeister is making me feel queasy.

The music gets a little louder.

SADHBH *turns around to look for* MATHILDE.

RONAN. Who are you looking for?

SADHBH. My assistant.

RONAN. She's fucked off with the young fella.

RONAN *notes* SADHBH*'s change of mood.*

You okay?

SADHBH *shrugs.*

SADHBH. Been a rough few weeks.

RONAN *pulls* SADHBH *in.*

RONAN. Don't go.

RONAN *snogs* SADHBH.

The music gets louder.

The party gets wilder and wilder until –

Music quietens.

SADHBH *is passed out on the couch. Some people leave the party.* MATHILDE (*drunk, stoned and emotional*) *is sitting beside* VIN (*who is off his face and is trying to roll a joint*).

VIN. There's gotta be purpose – / you know?

MATHILDE. Of course.

VIN. Purpose behind the image.
Iss the face. / Very powerful.
Yours iss… I'd kiss it if only one of them would stop moving.

They giggle and try to kiss.

MATHILDE. Face-power.

VIN. This is the baddest / shit.

MATHILDE. Bad is good.

VIN. Bad is superb.
The taxi driver / sold it to me.
The fucking taxi driver.

They explode with laughter.

MATHILDE. The taxi driver.

They laugh which turns into a giggle.

They giggle.

VIN. Suuuuperrrrb.

MATHILDE. Oh my God. I'm really whooo. (*Giggles.*) Really.
Wow. Hmm… I'd like to –
I mean I'm… (*Rubs* VIN's *arm.*)
I'm laughing. I haven't laughed for a month.

VIN. I'm drawn to conflict. (*Bursts out laughing.*)
And extremes of human experience. (*Laughs.*)

MATHILDE (*laughing*). So am I.

VIN *giggles at his badly made joint.*

I love your accent. Where are you from?

VIN. Tring.
Iss in Hertfordshire. (*Touches his heart.*)

MATHILDE. Trrrring – Hertfordshire England.
Oh my God – / beautiful.

VIN *passes* MATHILDE *a whiskey bottle, which she swigs from.*

VIN. I would like to live with you.
You're wunnerful.

MATHILDE. I have never had this much to drink in my life.
I've never had this much bad shit.

She giggles.

The Irish – they drink – fall down.
And then all is okay.

She strokes SADHBH*'s hair.* SADHBH *stirs a little.*

But / not me.

VIN. I'm okay. You're okay.
Can I live with you?

MATHILDE *giggles. She touches his hand.*

MATHILDE. I feel I would like to make love.

VIN *tries to light the joint.*

No. Don't try to light this –

They both giggle.

I warn you – I cry in my sleep.

Suddenly MATHILDE *cries.*

VIN. Hey. Hey.

He comforts her.

She takes the joint and tidies it up.

MATHILDE. I have so much stress. (*Stops crying and starts giggling uncontrollably.*)

VIN. I feel a bit – I'm a bit – What do you? You wanna – /
(*Rubs his face.*) it's my jaw… can't really feel it…

MATHILDE. If we fuck it doesn't have to be a big drama.

She lights the joint. She draws deeply.

VIN. And then we'll live together?

MATHILDE. Of course we'll leave together. You don't think I'm gonna fuck you right here on the floor? / We just have to get up the stairs.

They start to giggle.

VIN. No I mean – living – living.
You, me –

They giggle again.

MATHILDE. I don't know what you're saying. We go up the stairs? Stairs?

They giggle. MATHILDE *passes* VIN *the joint. He draws deeply.*

I'm a bit hairy. That might frighten you, English photographer from Tring.

MATHILDE *giggles.*

Or maybe it's sexy –

VIN *draws on the joint again.*

Yes. Let's fuck. But if you thought you know?
I could have a quick – If I could find a razor.

MATHILDE *giggles.*

MATHILDE *takes the joint.* VIN *finds himself in a bad way.*

VIN. Mathilde… I need to. Sorry. I'm not up to it… it's I – think I'm going to be –

VIN *dashes off to puke. He only manages to get to the back of the couch.*

He up-chucks to the end of the scene.

MATHILDE. Okay.
I don't need love.
I don't need LOVE to justify my existence.
I'm part of life you know.
It's all here.

Two

The following day.

The same space – which, in the light of day, is completely trashed.

SADHBH *is on the sofa and is extremely hung-over.*

INNOCENT *enters.*

INNOCENT. Excuse, madame. It's Innocent. I clean for
    Madame Romy.

SADHBH. Come in.

INNOCENT. *Pardonnez moi pour le retard. Ma soeur, elle est
    malade.*
    J'ai dû l'emmener à l'hôpital.

SADHBH. *Je suis désolée,* Innocent. I hope it's not serious.

INNOCENT. Please God, madame. / Please God.

SADHBH. I'm so sorry it's such a mess.
    Je vais t'aider.

    She gets up a little too quickly.

    Oh.

INNOCENT. Sit. Sit.
    Leave that for me.
    Je vais arranger ça pour Mme Romy.
    You have morning sickness. Yes?

SADHBH. What?

INNOCENT. I am the expert.
    I have seven children.
    I always know.

SADHBH. No, no. Not me.

From off.

STEPHEN. Hello? Hello?

INNOCENT. Yes, madame. I will make you a tisane.
Please one moment.

INNOCENT lets STEPHEN in and then backs out of the room.

SADHBH. You made it.

STEPHEN drops his bag and takes off his jacket.

STEPHEN. I saw them all on my way – the seekers, the preachers, profiteers, disaster junkies.

He leans over and kisses SADHBH.

SADHBH. Familiar faces then.
I almost don't recognise you in your suit.
You play the part well.

STEPHEN. This is me, Sadhbh. I am that guy in the suit.

He looks around.

Humanitarians by day – wannabe seventeen-year-olds by night.

SADHBH. One night is hardly living like seventeen-year-olds.

STEPHEN. There's vomit behind the couch.

SADHBH. Are you serious?

SADHBH gets up to have a look.

SADHBH tries to find something to clean up the mess.

It all got a bit out of hand.

STEPHEN. Sadhbh, it always gets a bit out of hand.
You know that.

SADHBH. I feel so awful.

STEPHEN. Have you not learned that R and R stands for rest and recreation?

SADHBH. Sweetheart, you sound middle-aged.

STEPHEN. Hoo-ray.
I'm delighted I'm not puking my ring up after an ICRC party.

SADHBH. How was your flight?

STEPHEN. Uncomfortable.
I hitched a ride on a UN Boeing. Unfortunately our pilot intends to fly back to Dar Es Salaam this evening.

SADHBH. You can't stay?

STEPHEN. I've got to be in London by Monday.

Pause.

I have a lunch at the Dutch Embassy.

SADHBH *is very disappointed.*

SADHBH. Of course you do.

STEPHEN. I have to be there. I hate it but, you know –

SADHBH. I hope you're teaching that unmentionable to be a good corporate citizen?

STEPHEN. Sure.

SADHBH. Do tell all about the Jolly Yellow Giant and its further misadventures in human rights?

STEPHEN. This conversation invariably ends in verbal – directed at me. Can we not…?

Pause.

Where's Romy?

SADHBH. At the clinic. We have the place to ourselves – and there is Mathilde, of course.

STEPHEN. How's she doing?

SADHBH. Better than I expected.

STEPHEN. I did wonder how she'd cope.

SADHBH. Cope? She's spent this morning having noisy sex with a young man she met last night – that only hours ago was barfing in the bathroom.

STEPHEN. Ah – banging and barfing – those were the days.

SADHBH. Do you want to go to bed? You look exhausted.

STEPHEN. I want to talk.

SADHBH. Okay.
Oh my – Oh –

SADHBH gags.

STEPHEN. You okay?

SADHBH. Jägermeister, beer – (*Gestures behind the couch.*) puke.

She gets up.

STEPHEN. Just leave it.

SADHBH. I can't have Innocent cleaning up puke.

STEPHEN. I'm sure he's cleaned up worse.

SADHBH. That is not my puke.

STEPHEN. I'm not sitting here with it steaming behind me. I've got a paper in my bag.

He goes to his briefcase.

Why don't I just – Are you okay?

SADHBH. Yeah.

STEPHEN lays some newspaper at the back of the couch.

He starts to pick up bits and pieces to clear a space for himself.

SADHBH lies back on the couch.

STEPHEN *sits beside her and she puts her head on his lap.*

She holds his hand.

Hello.

STEPHEN. Hello.

VIN *enters – barefoot, shirtless and wearing jeans – rubbing his chest and pulling at his hair.*

VIN. Morning.

STEPHEN *raises his hand in greeting.*

VIN *wanders around.*

I think – I left… my shit down here –

STEPHEN (*to* SADHBH). Not that as well.

SADHBH *starts to giggle.*

VIN *searches around* SADHBH *and* STEPHEN. *He reaches underneath* STEPHEN*'s legs.*

VIN. Sorry.

STEPHEN. You alright?

SADHBH. This it?

SADHBH *pulls a small pouch from the couch.*

VIN. Cool. Yeah.

He wanders off and then stops.

Do you guys want a smoke?

STEPHEN *and* SADHBH. No.

SADHBH. Thanks.

He wanders off.

VIN. No worries.

STEPHEN. Mathilde's playmate?

SADHBH. It appears so.

STEPHEN. What else have you been up to?

SADHBH. What do you mean?

STEPHEN. You've talked to Jerome Mburame.
Come on. Tell me.

SADHBH. He wanted to know if I had enough to indict him.

STEPHEN. I'm sure he's cacking himself.
I wish you had a sense of self-preservation.

SADHBH. He was not hostile.

STEPHEN. Not to you. You haven't got enough on him.

SADHBH. Yet. You're right. The women are afraid –
Many are in terrible physical state –
The brutality of the rapes… and then the psychological
damage. But the Mama – my contact at the camp – has found
witnesses who want to talk to me.

STEPHEN. That's a result.

SADHBH. The thing is – I feel – in a way – he's been warned.

STEPHEN. No, Sadhbh – *you've* been warned.
So how long will this investigation take?

SADHBH. How long is a piece of string?

STEPHEN. You said three months max.

SADHBH. And I meant it, but I have a responsibility here.

STEPHEN. There are plenty of other researchers.

SADHBH. Yes but they're local and you know they face
intimidation and violence in the way that I don't. Now that
Bibi has left I'm the most senior researcher.

STEPHEN. I came here today with an agenda.

SADHBH. I'm a bit afraid.

STEPHEN. Don't be.

SADHBH. Do you want to leave me?

STEPHEN. You're the one who leaves.
I've been offered a six-month contract in Beijing.
$85,000 plus per diems plus an apartment.

SADHBH. Holy fuck. Wow.
Does this have anything to do with your lunch / at the Dutch Embassy?

STEPHEN. I need to be able to indicate my interest. /
I don't want to go without you.

SADHBH. Oh. Oh.
I see. I see.
China is hardly my area / of expertise.

STEPHEN. You were serious about stopping fieldwork?

SADHBH. I didn't say I'd stop working.

STEPHEN. You've changed your mind?

SADHBH. There is a little girl. Amala. I made her a promise.

STEPHEN. You're using that as an excuse?

SADHBH. Fuck right off.

STEPHEN *shakes his head.*

Why are you shaking your head?

STEPHEN. There's always going to be an Amala, or the little boy or the fourteen-year-old or the thirty-five-year-old, or the elderly lady or the dying man –

SADHBH. I know.

STEPHEN. – but there won't always be me.

SADHBH. So you keep threatening.

SADHBH *thumps* STEPHEN.

STEPHEN. I'm not threatening – (*Fends off her thump.*)
I am serious.

SADHBH *thumps him again.*

Hit me again and I'll hit you back.

STEPHEN *stops* SADHBH.

He holds down her arms.

I'll finally be in a decent financial situation.
We could think about a home not an apartment.
Having a family –
Six months together is what / we need.

SADHBH. It's still six months in China taking dirty money.

STEPHEN. For fuck's sake, Sadhbh – grow up!
These are our lives! Our lives.
We either spend them apart –

SADHBH. I'll think.

STEPHEN. – or together – not this in-between.

SADHBH. I'll think. I'll think.

STEPHEN. I need more than that. I need an answer.
Before I get on the plane tonight.

Silence. SADHBH *looks away.*

STEPHEN *gets up and gets a glass of water. He drinks a little.*

He takes off his jacket and opens the top buttons on his shirt.

He runs his hand across the back of his neck – the heat starting to get to him.

SADHBH. What's your start date?

STEPHEN. Six weeks' time.

SADHBH *gets up and moves away. She experiences a wave of nausea.*

She gets a glass of water.

Dicky tummy still?

SADHBH. I need to eat – but I can't face food.

SADHBH *breaks down and cries.*

STEPHEN. Hey.

He moves to SADHBH *and puts his arms around her.*

Darling – you're just tired.

He holds her tightly.

I'm sorry, I'm sorry, I'm sorry.
Pressure, pressure, eh?

SADHBH. Obviously I wouldn't be able to come for the first
month –
I could probably get a leave of absence for the rest of the
time. Of course I could.

STEPHEN. I could live with that.

SADHBH. Are you absolutely serious?
Yes,

STEPHEN. Why was that easier than I / thought it would be?

He puts his arms around her.

SADHBH. Just shut up.
Oh, you smelt so sweet when you arrived.

STEPHEN. I smell of vomit?

SADHBH. Maybe – a little splash.

INNOCENT *enters with tea. He stops for a moment, not
knowing whether to turn and leave the room or deliver the
tea.*

STEPHEN. Come in, Innocent.

INNOCENT. Of course, Papa.

INNOCENT *puts the tea things in front of* SADHBH.

Désirez-vous du thé, Papa?

STEPHEN. *Plus tard, peut-être,* Innocent. Thank you.
(*To* SADHBH) I need to freshen up. Two minutes.

He leaves the room.

INNOCENT. Madame?

SADHBH. Thank you, Innocent.

INNOCENT. *Madame est fatiguée. Madame doit aller se coucher.*

SADHBH. Thank you. *C'est une bonne idée.*

INNOCENT. *C'est la chaleur. Il fait très lourd. En tout cas* – it will rain tonight.

INNOCENT *pours* SADHBH *some tea.* INNOCENT *hands her the cup. He starts to tidy up.*

Please, madame.

SADHBH *sips some tea and lies back on the sofa.* INNOCENT *cleans.*

Three

That night. Same space.

MATHILDE *enters.* SADHBH *is resting.*

MATHILDE. You're in the dark too.

SADHBH. Power cut.
I can give you some candles to take to your room.

SADHBH *lights a lamp.*

MATHILDE. I'm wondering if –

SADBH. Yeah?

MATHILDE. Someone can? A friend –

SADHBH. The guy you were giving mouth-to-mouth last night?

MATHILDE. It's my fault Vin missed his trip.

SADHBH. You tied him up? Forced him to drink a bottle of
whiskey?

MATHILDE. Ah, okay. And we're going to Masisi and he needs
to go –

SADHBH. Tell him to meet here at 7:45 tomorrow morning.
Janvier is arriving at 8.

MATHILDE. Oh, thank you.

SADHBH. Are you still hanging?

MATHILDE. What is 'hanging'?

SADHBH. Do you still feel shite?

MATHILDE. Very, very shite. Yes,
You?

SADHBH. Sick as a dog.
Terrible nausea. All day.

MATHILDE. Poor you.
And Stephen? He caught his flight.

SADHBH. Yeah. He's gone.

MATHILDE. Ah – I'm sorry for that.

SADHBH *shrugs*.

SADHBH. This is not a good job for relationships.

MATHILDE. I have noticed in our programme – no one has
kids. Most women are single.

SADHBH. Not everyone wants '*la vie bourgeoise*'!

MATHILDE. But – for me –
Take Bibi –

SADHBH. What about Bibi?

MATHILDE. I don't want to be like her.
No home, no children and now she's ill and old.

SADHBH. She's thirty-seven.

MATHILDE *looks at her uncomprehendingly.*

MATHILDE. *Pourquoi tu est triste?*

SADHBH. Because I am.

MATHILDE. I think it's wonderful you go to China together. An adventure, ah?

SADHBH. Yeah – to Beijing – that well-known haven for human rights activists.

MATHILDE *does not know what to say for a moment.*

SADHBH *fans herself with her hat. She groans.*

MATHILDE. You are unwell a lot.

SADHBH. I'm not unwell. I'm pregnant.

MATHILDE. What?

SADHBH. Yeah.

MATHILDE. How do you know?

SADHBH. I've missed a period. My boobs are sore, I'm perpetually queasy. And I just did a test with Romy.

MATHILDE. Oh my God – but that's so –
Congratulations. Oh, beautiful.

SADHBH *says nothing – but she allows herself a smile.*

So… You did not know this at the party?

SADHBH. I had an idea. Romy confirmed it.

MATHILDE. Because you had a lot of – the stuff that numbs the brain –

SADHBH. Don't. I know.

MATHILDE. Is Stephen happy?

SADHBH. Too many questions, Mathilde.

MATHILDE. Sorry but –

SADHBH. I'm just six weeks gone. It feels more like indigestion than a baby.

MATHILDE. You didn't tell him?

SADHBH. He'd have made me go back with him.
　　I didn't want that. We have a job to do here.

MATHILDE. It's not very hygienic – where we go.
　　And there is cholera in Lushabere.
　　Perhaps it is better if you go –

SADHBH. Mathilde! There is no one but us to finish this
　　investigation.
　　If we work our asses off and interview ten people a day
　　we'll be home in a month.

MATHILDE. I'm happy for that.

SADHBH. But we go when we've got enough to put the
　　frighteners on Mburame and not before.

MATHILDE. But you can't ignore –

SADHBH. Did you want something else?

MATHILDE. No.

SADHBH. Go on. Spend time with –

MATHILDE. Vin. He is asleep now.
　　He threw up all night.
　　But we've had sex – so I'm happy…

SADHBH. Good. Good for you.

MATHILDE. It's just been good to get a break – from the
　　guilt.

SADHBH. Go. Wake him up. Enjoy it.
　　From now on you'll never escape the feeling you've failed
　　someone.
　　And you will have.

　　SADHBH *throws her arm over* MATHILDE's *shoulder.*
　　MATHILDE *leans into* SADHBH.

　　Sounds of the city. After some moments the atmospheric
　　sounds segue into the sounds from the compound.

Four

The compound.

A cow lows loudly. VIN *is taking photographs.* MATHILDE *is wearing a bikini top and cut-off shorts.*

MATHILDE. Hey, boy from Tring! You can't just leave me alone in bed. What is that?

VIN. It's commonly known as a cow.

MATHILDE. Of course I know this.
But why is? Where does it come from?

VIN. Democratic Republic of Congo?

MATHILDE. Vin!

VIN. It's a gift – for Madame 'Kavanagh'.
From Colonel Mburame.
A great compliment apparently.

MATHILDE. No. This can't be true.

VIN. I think you'll find it is true.

The cow lows.

Two scary blokes delivered it this morning.

MATHILDE. *Merde. Une vache.*
And I smell its shit.

Regarde – there is cow poop everywhere.

SADHBH *enters.*

Disgusting.

SADHBH. I think Mburame is trying to make me feel at home.

VIN. Sadhbh and Mburame up a / tree. K-I-S-S-I –

SADHBH. Exactly how old / are you, Vin?

MATHILDE. That is terrible. You / can't accept it.
It must go back.

SADHBH. Strap her on the back of a motorcycle?
Squeeze her / into the Jeep?

MATHILDE. Why are you smiling?
Mburame has given you a – cow.
Does he think he can bribe you?

SADHBH. Do I look like a woman who can be / bribed with a
cow?

The cow lows.

SADHBH *laughs.*

MATHILDE. Stop laughing. For me – this is terrible.
He is a monster. /
You have blood on your hands.

SADHBH. Steady now. Steady.
It's very easy to categorise such people as evil. Mburame is
an evil man who does evil things therefore he is less human.
If faced with the things he's faced, / let's hope we would not
become killers.

MATHILDE. I can't believe you can say this after Amala and
all the women and –

SADHBH. Just for a moment think like a grown-up.

The cow lows.

MATHILDE. What?

VIN. I am so doing cow jokes all day.
Sacré vache! Classic.
La vache qui rit.

He takes a photograph.

SADHBH. Don't.
If I ever see a picture of me and that / cow in any publication –

VIN. Don't have a cow.

SADHBH. Mathilde.
You're right to think it's sinister.
Radio trottoir will ensure everyone knows about Mburame's
gift of 'friendship'.
But while we are so cut off here – it's a bad idea to spurn him.

MATHILDE *is visibly annoyed.*

MATHILDE. But of course I'm being stupid again.

SADHBH. No need to call the righteous brigade every time
something happens.
You won't cope here always living on your nerves.

MATHILDE. So you say –
but if we keep it – this looks like collaboration.
Isn't that a 'bad idea'?

SADHBH. Either way – there's no winning.

MATHILDE. Okay. Thank you. That's clear.

SADHBH *makes to leave.*

Oh my God. It is pooping again.

SADHBH. Forget about it.

MATHILDE. Where are you going?

SADHBH. To get a bucket.
That cow needs to be milked.
You want to get dressed? It's not the Costa del Sol.
We leave for the camp in an hour.

SADHBH *exits and calls back.*

R and R is officially over.

MATHILDE *sulks.*

The cow lows a number of times.

VIN *takes a photograph.*

Five

The IDP camp.

Tight spot of light.

A small CHILD *is screaming.* VIN *is taking a photograph of the* CHILD. *The* CHILD *tries to get away but seems pinned to the spot.*

VIN *follows her face with his camera.*

CHILD. The Gun, The Gun, The Gun, The Gun, The Gun.

VIN. Hey, little one. It's a camera
    Camera?
    I'm taking a photograph.
    Je prends ta photo?
    You want to have a look?
    Hey, don't cry, kid.
    I'm sorry.
    I can show you.
    Hey. Shush. Shush.
    Kid? Can you stop crying please?
    You'll get me in trouble.
    Kid? Please?

He turns his camera around to view the images.

See. I can show you.

The CHILD *runs away.*

Shit.

He looks back at the images on his camera.

SADHBH. What the fuck are you doing?

VIN. Listen – sorry – I didn't mean to –

    MATHILDE *and* MAMA CAROLINA *enter.*

SADHBH. You are not allowed to photograph or talk to the children without Mama Carolina's permission. The last time they had something pointed at them it was a gun. They're traumatised. / You just can't behave like that.

MATHILDE. Hey, Sadhbh – he / didn't mean to –

MAMA CAROLINA. Why have you upset the children?

VIN. Hey, Mama, / I didn't mean to.

MAMA CAROLINA. My name is not Mama. I am Mama Carolina.

SADHBH. Ask permission if / you want pictures.

MATHILDE. This is a misunderstanding –

MAMA CAROLINA. *Prends ton appareil et va-t-en. Va-t-en !*

MATHILDE. Sorry, Mama Carolina –

VIN. Okay. I'll just go then.

SADHBH. Fuck off. / Go on. Fuck off.

MATHILDE. Cool it, Sadhbh.

VIN. Keep your hair on. I didn't mean / to upset anyone.

VIN gathers his equipment and moves away to pack up.

MAMA CAROLINA. *Pourquoi parles-tu comme ça, Sadhbh? On est devant les enfants, quand même?* Now – please – we are waiting for you.

She exits.

SADHBH. Sorry, Mama Carolina. *Pardonne-moi. En moment.*

SADHBH *and* MATHILDE *are left alone together.*

He's an idiot.

MATHILDE. I'm sorry. It's not my fault.

SADHBH. It is your fault. You brought this guy. He's sleeping in your bed. Suddenly we're responsible for his security – Janvier is / not his chaffeur.

MATHILDE. I'm sorry but no, Sadhbh.
He is taking truthful pictures. / Powerful pictures.

SADHBH. How can you say that? You know him for about five minutes! The guy only cares to makes a name for himself.

MATHILDE. And so what if he can make people look?

SADHBH. He asked Mama Carolina to show him the raped children? / It's not on.

MATHILDE. What do you want me to do?

SADHBH. He can't stay with us any longer.

MATHILDE. What will he do?

SADHBH. I don't know. It's not my problem.
Why is that my problem?

MATHILDE. It's becoming unsettled just beyond Masisi. Outbreaks of violence in the hills. There are rumours / in the camp.

SADHBH. Tell him to collect his stuff. I'll arrange security back to Goma.

MATHILDE. The room at the compound is my own, is it not?

SADHBH. It is.

MATHILDE. So – in fact – it's not your business.

SADHBH. You could say that.

MATHILDE. I think your hormones are making you very aggressive.

SADHBH. Fuck the hormones – I am aggressive.

Pause.

I'm sorry if I'm being harsh but we're trying to build up the kids' trust here. / That's the most important thing.

MATHILDE. I understand – of course I know this. Why do you always talk to me like I'm stupid?

SADHBH. I don't. / Mathilde?

MATHILDE. Yes. Yes. Yes. We all can't be like you! Without a
life.
You'll have to start without me.

Vin?

SADHBH *shakes her head and moves away.*

VIN *approaches* MATHILDE.

VIN. Hey. Sorry. (*Takes her hand.*)

MATHILDE. Not now.

VIN. I've no way of getting back to the compound. What does
she –

MATHILDE. Don't take pictures of the kids around here.
This is her territory.

VIN. I've taken / barely anything.

MATHILDE. She's being totally unreasonable.

VIN. Bit of a boot.

MATHILDE (*giggles*). Shush.

VIN *kisses* MATHILDE.

VIN. If I'm going to show stuff it's got to be serious work.
Hey – that letter you told me about.
The invitation from Colonel Mburame.
If I could get a portrait of him –

MATHILDE. That sounds like a really bad idea.

VIN. He sent her a cow, didn't he?
And she said he was perfectly civilised.

MATHILDE. No. She said he gave her tea.

VIN. Exactly.
And I know just how to do it.
Him on a chair. Staring down the barrel of the lens.
Bam.
I'll whack the picture off to Reuters as soon as.

MATHILDE. Vin.

VIN. Come on.
I'll borrow one of the cars and go early in the morning. In fact, Janvier can take me. He'll know where to go. We'll be there and back before anyone's up.

MATHILDE. Vin. There are nine hundred and seventy-eight men, women and children living in shit here. The serious work is in front of you.
Now
Do as she says. Fuck off. Take pictures.

They kiss. The light fades.

Six

We hear gunfire and chaos as in the Prologue.

As the light fades on the scene we hear the Prologue scene dialogue through a walkie-talkie radio.

There are shouts of panic.

The door is kicked. Once. Twice.

SADHBH. *Mon Dieu, pitié.*

SOLDIER. *La ferme!*

SADHBH. *Je m'appelle Sadhbh, et ça c'est Mathilde.*
Nous avons de l'argent. Beaucoup des dollars.
Je vous en prie!

MATHILDE. *Nous avons des cigarettes.*

SADHBH. *Je vous en prie. Prenez tout.*

SOLDIER. *Mettez vous par terre. Tout de suite.*
Accroupies.

SADHBH. *Nous avons du whisky. Prenez-le. Prenez –le, buvez le avec vos enfants.*

SOLDIER. *Déshabillez-vous.*

MATHILDE. *Non, non, je vous en prie. Nous sommes mariées, nous sommes mères.*

SOLDIER. *Déshabillez-vous.*

MATHILDE. *Non, non, non.*

SADHBH. *Je peux vous donner l'argent.*
Nous avons presque quatre mille dollars.
Prenez-les. C'est pour vous.
Dieu vous pardonnera, si vous partez maintenant.

SOLDIER. *Je prends l'argent.*
Je prends les téléphones.
Je prends tout.
Et, ensuite, je vais terminer le boulot.

MATHILDE *starts to cry.*

On ne vous entend pas.
Personne ne vous écoute.

The shadows close in.

Seven

A bar. Goma.

Sweltering heat. Blinding sun and blue sky.

RONAN *is interviewing* SADHBH. *He has a recording device but also takes notes on his Mac.*

She fans herself with her hat. She is bruised and sore. RONAN *is drinking a Primus beer.* SADHBH *is drinking a Coke.* RONAN *shows her the recording device.*

RONAN. Okay?

SADHBH. If you must.

RONAN. This attack on your compound must have been
    traumatic –

SADHBH. I investigate war crimes and crimes against
    humanity committed by some dangerous individuals and that
    inevitably means I step on a lot of toes.
    I've received death threats – the odd brick though the door.
    It's par for the course.
    After nearly eight years here – I felt I'd the measure of the
    Congolese. Obviously falsely so.

RONAN. Can you tell me what happened? Is that okay, Sadhbh?
    Just tell me the story in your own time.

SADHBH. 6 a.m. Tuesday – our compound came under attack
    by rebel combatants.

RONAN. You've been ruffling the feathers of Jerome
    Mburame.

SADHBH. They were not wearing identifiable uniforms.

RONAN. It's the most likely –

SADHBH. There is no evidence, Ronan.
    Not a shred to say Tutsi, Hutu, Mai Mai. Mburame.
    It was violence. A way of life here.
    I could give your readers a lecture on violent practices
    introduced under colonialism, but I reckon you want
    something short and pithy.

    Pause.

RONAN. Your security guard was killed.

SADHBH. Janvier Nizaine – I've known him for –

    She stops for a moment unable to speak.

    And a young British journalist Vincent Holman.
    We think the attackers followed him on his return to the
    compound. They shot him in the arm when he didn't have
    the $100 they were demanding.

RONAN. His injuries are serious but not life threatening.

SADHBH. That's what I've heard too.
He and another colleague who suffered a serious assault
were flown to Joburg.
I escaped with minor injuries.

RONAN. A fractured rib – severe bruising?
Not at / all minor.

SADHBH. I'm okay. Really. I'm okay.

RONAN. The serious assault.
This happened to your colleague Mathilde Rolla.
She suffered a sexual assault.

SADHBH. What? Switch that thing off.

RONAN. Sure. Are you okay?

SADHBH. Jesus, Ronan. Come on. I can't talk about that.
We agreed.

He stops recording.

RONAN. Everyone knows about it, Sadhbh –

SADHBH. No way.

RONAN. People should know about the kind of danger you're
exposed to out here.

SADHBH. It's not my story to tell.
Why would I tell / you about it?

RONAN. But it is your story.

Silence.

I want to give you a chance to give your account of the
attack. There are so many rumours.

SADHBH *shakes her head.*

SADHBH. There are always rumours in Congo.
Radio trottoir. 'Radio of the pavement.'

SADHBH *passes her hand across her forehead. She is
feverish.*

RONAN. Do you want to stop for a minute?
Take a break? You say.

SADHBH. On the record. For the benefit of your readers.

He resumes recording…

Go to Google and look up 'humanitarian worker, human
rights defender'. You'll find articles that include kidnapping,
injury, robbery, rape, shooting, murder. The threat to safety
and security is very real.
Of course you want to make a difference but you don't do
this job for the recognition and you definitely don't do it for
the money.
It's serious stuff.

Pause.

I'm done.

RONAN *stops recording.*

RONAN. Are you okay? You're very pale.

SADHBH. The heat is something else.

RONAN. Are you heading back to London this evening?

SADHBH *nods.*

SADHBH. I'll be home in time for the ten o'clock news
tomorrow night.

RONAN. Can I get you another drink? A water?

SADHBH. Not for me.

RONAN. What are you going to do? Will you come back to
Congo?

SADHBH. I don't know.

Pause.

Courage is a bit like a bank balance.
Debit too much and you go in the red.
I'm in the red.

RONAN *stretches out his hand to* SADHBH.

RONAN. Can I quote you on that?

SADHBH. No.

RONAN. I'm always afraid here.
   Can't fucking wait to get back to Dublin.
   I've never really understood your attachment to Congo.
   Poor Sadhbh. You thought you were untouchable here.

SADHBH. I'm not going to be your *New York Times* story and
   you're pissed off, Ronan.

RONAN. Not at all. I'm amazed at your reluctance to talk. This
   is a victim-based account of a crisis. / Surely it's what you
   do day in and day out here?

SADHBH. I'm not a victim.

RONAN. You've become a victim of the very thing you're
   investigating. But if you're going to stand in the line of fire –

SADHBH. Stop. Just stop there, Ronan.

RONAN. I'm sorry, Sadhbh. I'm really desperately sorry for
   what has happened to you.

SADHBH. I know your angle.
   I guess a raped humanitarian will get many more inches than
   a raped eight-year-old Congolese girl. Where were you when
   fifty-three women and girls were raped in Masisi?
   Or is that too much of a norm to appear in the *New York
   Times*?

RONAN. We're locked into a relationship whether you like it or
   not.
   You give me a story. I bring it to the public.
   You get focus on Congo.
   Your organisation gets more recognition.
   Mutual responsibility, Sadhbh.

SADHBH. Screw you.
   I want to see a copy of this article before it goes to print.

   SADHBH *stands up*.

RONAN. You've been through a hell of an ordeal.
I knew that little chancer who was shot too.
It's a shock – you know – Jesus – it's a shock. I'm just
saying –
For all of us –

They look at one another.

There but for the grace of –
What's that?

SADHBH. What?

There is a small pool of blood on the chair.

RONAN. The blood.

SADHBH. That's me. That's me, isn't it?

Eight

Ireland.

Brennan's Bar. Donegal.

Five months later.

A flight landing which leads into a long note from a fiddle which develops into a traditional air. A banner is hung.

'HAPPY 30TH BIRTHDAY SADHBH'

We're at a party. A group dance (a Siege of Ennis or some such) with SADHBH *in the middle. They clap her and whirl her and then dance off – taking the banner.*

The sound in the background is that of the party – on stage is of the street.

A lorry rumbles near by. SADHBH *is at the back of Brennan's Bar and has been followed by* BIBI *and* MATHILDE. *A neon sign of Brennan's illuminates the small scene.*

MATHILDE. Hey!

BIBI. What's he doing here?

SADHBH. This is kind of overwhelming.
Look – he called the day before yesterday – said he wanted –
needed – to see me. /
I didn't think he'd come straight away.

MATHILDE. He was shocked to see us. Did you see that?

BIBI. Are you surprised? I love the guy but / he's acted like a
jerk.

SADHBH. Please just be yourself with him.
I didn't tell him you guys were coming over for my birthday.
He thought – I was going to be alone.
You know – we've been calling, / emailing. It's okay.

BIBI. If I 'be myself' with him I'll kick his ass – but under the
circumstances –

MATHILDE. We will be so cool.

SADHBH. Thank you.

She puts her arms around MATHILDE.

MATHILDE. I mean – we'll get drunk tonight? You're not too
old for that.

SADHBH. Never.

MATHILDE. Okay. He's coming.

STEPHEN *stands away a little*.

BIBI. I love Kincasslagh. It's like the twenty-first century hasn't
got this far north.
People say things like 'Enjoy the power of the Atlantic'.
Beautiful.

SADHBH. They just might be putting it on.

BIBI. No. Because I'm American?

SADHBH. Because you're a tourist.

BIBI. No way! Don't spoil it.

SADHBH. What can I say? You guys paid for a sea view – on Cruit Island. You're surrounded by the 'power of the Atlantic'.

MATHILDE. I'm afraid we did.

BIBI. Okay, total suckers for the 'blarney'.

SADHBH. Have you walked along the Tra Dearg?
Roughly translates as the Red Strand.

BIBI. Take us tomorrow.

SADHBH. There's a beautiful walk from your cottage.
On a clear day you might see the outline of Tory Island. The last outpost of Gaelic civilisation.

BIBI. Oh my God! You're doing it too. That blarney stuff.

SADHBH. Underneath it all – we're actually Leprechauns.

STEPHEN. Hi!
Can we talk?

MATHILDE. Hey. Sure, Stephen.

BIBI. We'll see you inside?

Pause.

SADHBH. Brilliant. See you in a minute.

MATHILDE. Hurry. I want to learn the jig.

MATHILDE *turns back and kisses* SADHBH *four times.*

The women exit. SADHBH *and* STEPHEN *are alone together.*

SADHBH. I haven't seen Mathilde since Congo.
Her second HIV test was clear, thank God.

STEPHEN. I guessed as much. But that's good news. Great. Great. She's getting on with it.

SADHBH. We all are. It's not something can be fixed.

STEPHEN *nods*.

STEPHEN. Bibi's a little cool with me.

SADHBH. It's your imagination.

STEPHEN. You think?

Pause.

I hired a van from London so I brought all your stuff with me.

SADHBH. It would have fit in a rucksack but that's really kind.

STEPHEN. It is and it isn't.

Pause.

I'm leasing the flat – or hoping I can.

SADHBH. That was quick.

STEPHEN. I've taken another contract in China. Twelve months.

SADHBH. Have you moved your Chinese translator into our flat?

STEPHEN. Course not.

Pause.

No. Susie is still in Beijing.

SADHBH. Is she a fuck-up too?

STEPHEN. She leaves that to me.

Pause.

How are you doing?

SADHBH. My mother is driving me crazy. She doesn't understand the concept 'leave of absence'.
I'm trying to write up the report from Masisi.
She's telling everyone I've moved home.

STEPHEN. You didn't have to come back to Ireland.
You could have stayed in the flat until you found a place.

SADHBH. Of course I had to fucking come back.
I didn't want to be a lodger in my own home.
Could you not have waited for me to come out to Beijing?

STEPHEN. It was clear you didn't want to come.

SADHBH. Horseshit. I took a leave of absence, didn't I?
You knew I had to tie things up in London.
It took you all of five minutes to meet someone.

STEPHEN. It was clear you thought nothing about me or us.

SADHBH. How can you say that? I was recovering –

STEPHEN. I'm talking about our baby. You didn't tell me.

SADHBH. I was six weeks pregnant, Stephen. That's not a baby!

STEPHEN. You didn't want it.

SADHBH. You don't know that!
How can you say that?
The truth is we moved so far from each other –
You just didn't have the balls to say it before you left for Beijing.

STEPHEN. Why didn't you have the balls to say it?
Sadhbh, we have always wanted different things –

SADHBH. You just want ordinary, Stephen.

STEPHEN. I want peace. I don't want to be part of your appetite for chaos.

SADHBH. So you've punished me,
I'm punished, Stephen.
I'm up to fucking here with guilt.
What are you here for anyway?
Who asked you?
We've screamed what we had to scream at one another.

STEPHEN. Over the phone.

SADHBH. I don't want to go through it again.
Enough. Enough. Enough.

Pause.

STEPHEN. This is awful. I'm so sorry.

SADHBH. I thought I could do it.
It's just – stupid – isn't it?

She shakes her head.

STEPHEN. I'm leaving tomorrow.
Sorry. I really wanted to see you before I go back to Beijing.

SADHBH. You've seen me.

Pause.

I know. I wanted to see you too.
It's my fault. I should have said no.

STEPHEN. But we're not ready –
And
I've really missed you.
Badly. Badly.

SADHBH. I'm fine.
Let's just try and cope with this evening.

STEPHEN. Sorry. Of course.

SADHBH. You should go in. Mum will only be scourging me
about you tomorrow. She thinks tonight is the big
reconciliation. Don't want to give her the wrong idea.

STEPHEN. No.

SADHBH. You go on – I'm gonna –
I'll just be a few minutes.

STEPHEN. Okay.

He takes a page of folded magazine from his back pocket.

I thought this might interest you.

She looks at the page.

Vincent Holman. He's the photographer who –

SADHBH. I know who he is.

STEPHEN. He won the Ian Parry award –

SADHBH. For 'The Gun, The Gun, The Gun'.
The little shit.
Don't mention Vin to Mathilde.

STEPHEN. Course.

SADHBH. Can I keep this?

STEPHEN. I brought it for you.

Beat.

Do you think you'll go back? To Congo?

SADHBH. What does it matter to you?

STEPHEN. Because I'll be worried? I'll always be worried.

He turns to exit.

I think a lot about us and what could have been and the
baby… It's not like I don't think about it.
I think about you.

SADHBH *nods.* STEPHEN *exits.*

SADHBH *lights up a cigarette. The wind picks up. She pulls
her jacket tightly around herself.*

After some moments a man about the same age joins her.

MICHAEL. How are ya?

SADHBH. Michael Pender. Howya yerself?

MICHAEL. Brass monkey weather wha?

SADHBH. I'm willing the east wind away.

MICHAEL. Gis one.

She hands him a cigarette and he lights it from her lit cigarette.

Welcome to the leper colony.
There's only a few of us left.

They stand about – dragging hard on cigarettes.

Haven't seen you for years.

SADHBH *shrugs*.

SADHBH. About five years, is it?

MICHAEL. Naw. More like ten.

SADHBH. Is it?

MICHAEL. It is.
Yer ma knows how to throw a do.

SADHBH. Ah, ya know Cait Kavanagh. Was she looking for me?

MICHAEL. Yer grand. She's forcing ham sandwiches on your vegetarian friends at the moment. Really good to see ya, Sadhbh.
You haven't changed a bit.

SADHBH. Ya think?

MICHAEL. Ya look exactly the same as when you'd stride up main street to meet me. The hair flyin' and yer Stetson pulled nearly over yer eyes.
They used to call you the cowboy of Kincasslagh.
Did you know that?

SADHBH. No, I didn't.

She laughs.

The cowboy of Kincasslagh.

Pause.

You've not changed.

MICHAEL. Go on outta that. I'm the same apart from the
    paunch and a thin spot the baby calls 'a hole in yer head,
    Daddy'.

SADHBH. How old's the baby?

MICHAEL. Ciara is four, nearly five. Well, not so much a baby
    any more but sure Fintan is nearly nine.

SADHBH. Wow.

MICHAEL. And we're expecting our third in a couple of weeks.
    That's why Karen didn't come.

SADHBH. How is she?

MICHAEL. Big as a house.
    Asking after ya.

SADHBH. I'm surprised.

MICHAEL. I think she realises after marriage, three kids and a
    Mitsubishi Shogun – I ain't going anywhere.

SADHBH. We only went out at school.

MICHAEL. Ah, but ya see – you were my first love.

SADHBH. Was I?

MICHAEL. Broke my heart. Yep.
    You lost your accent!

SADHBH. Sorry about that.

MICHAEL. Ya did well to get out of this town.
    I still see the old crowd.
    I'm still working for the da.
    Still drinkin' at The Railway bar.
    You know, same old, same old.
    Do you keep in touch with any of the girls?

SADHBH. No. No, I don't.

MICHAEL. Ah well. They're all about anyhow.

SADHBH. How's your da's business? Did the recession bite?

MICHAEL. Ah – but we'll manage. We always do.

SADHBH. Glad to hear it.

MICHAEL. So, eh – Africa hah?
We saw ya on a news programme about Darfur.

SADHBH. I was in Congo.

MICHAEL. Yeah, no. Good stuff. You were working with all
those refugees.

SADHBH. Internally displaced people. I was.

MICHAEL. You don't hear so much about the Congo now.
Has the situation improved at all?

SADHBH. It's a catastrophe.

MICHAEL. Jesus. Pardon my ignorance.

SADHBH. Don't worry about it.
It doesn't make the news much.

MICHAEL. Even at school it was clear you were going to
cannonball your way there.

SADHBH. I had a notion I could save the continent.

MICHAEL. And we believed ya.
Remember ten pee for the black babies at school.

SADHBH. There was a felt board.
And for every pound collected we built up a picture of an
African village. A pound for a hut –

RONAN. A pound for a palm tree,
you were forever scourgin' us to hand over our pocket money.

SADHBH. Ten pee for the black babies sounds a bit dubious
now.

MICHAEL. Ah, yeah. The nuns wouldn't get away with that
now.
Then again – there's a lot the nuns wouldn't get away with
now.
So –
Did you figure it out?

SADHBH. Figure out what?

MICHAEL. Why can't Africa look after Africa?

SADHBH is about to answer and then stops herself.

SADHBH. Haven't a clue. But at heart – I'm an optimist.

MICHAEL. The town's very proud of ya, Sadhbh.
Ya know? Yer truly a citizen of the world.
Doing something – the kind of stuff ya would think about but would never do.
You've earned your title.

SADHBH. Cowboy of Kincasslagh?

MICHAEL. Fair fucks to you.
Listen, would ya ever think of coming up to The Railway one of the nights? It's the old crowd but they'd love to see ya.

SADHBH. Oh, well… that's, eh – I'm writing up a / report and –

MICHAEL. It's just if you wanted to like.

SADHBH. Yeah.

Pause.

MICHAEL. Is that your fella in there?

Pause.

SADHBH. No.

MICHAEL. You had to think about that, didn't ya.

SADHBH. I did.

There is a silence.

MICHAEL *pushes a strand of hair from her face.*

The music starts up again.

SADHBH*'s name is being called from off.*

MICHAEL. It's the last dance of the night.

Pause.

Might you have the last dance with me?

SADHBH. Tongues will wag.

MICHAEL. I'll chance it.

SADHBH *stubs out her cigarette.*

SADHBH. I better go in.

MICHAEL. Well, come on then, Miss Kavanagh.
This is your life.

MICHAEL *takes her hand and twirls her around.*

Bright spot of light.

The Congolese SOLDIER *appears. He raises his AK-47
towards* SADHBH.

SOLDIER. *Je vais terminer le boulot.*

End of Act Two.

EPILOGUE

Congo.

The IDP camp.

Children's drawings of conflict stuck on a fence.

MAMA CAROLINA. *Tu es enfin revenue. Dieu soit loué.*
Et où es la petite Française?

SADHBH. She said to tell Mama Carolina and all the children
that she loves you and thinks of you all every day.

MAMA CAROLINA. *Qu'elle soit bénie.* She was very
agreeable with the children. I ask because a young nurse
from Médecins sans Frontières shows me an article from the
New York Times. We have worried about her.

SADHBH. Mathilde is now based at our Paris headquarters.

MAMA CAROLINA. I think *la petite Française* will not return.
This is a great sadness.
Poor Congo.

SADHBH. This is true. This is true.
And tell me – how is Amala?

MAMA CAROLINA. She does not cry so much these last
months and she is one of the fortunate ones.
She does not have HIV. But I must tell you – in a camp like
this – there are many rumours.
What happens if Mburame is not convicted?

SADHBH. The prosecutor believes they're going to make an
example of Colonel Jerome Mburame. It'll have enormous
impact.

MAMA CAROLINA. I am still frightened for Amala.

SADHBH. I will look after Amala.
I will make sure she is not identified.

MAMA CAROLINA. She has been waiting for you. One moment.
Amala? Amala? Come this instant.
She has been practising her English.

AMALA *runs in carrying a home-made gun.*

She throws herself at SADHBH.

AMALA. Mama Sadhbh, Mama Sadhbh.
Tu es revenue!

SADHBH. *Oui, te l'avais promis.*

AMALA. *Regarde – moi, je suis grosse.*
Je suis Américaine.
I want to be like you when I grow up.
Give me your sky piece.

SADHBH *gives* AMALA *her hat.* AMALA *puts it on and runs around and around. She points the gun.*

Je suis Mama Sadhbh.
Je suis Américaine.
Je suis Irlandaise.
Je suis.
Je suis.
I am Amala.
I am Amala.
I will tell all the stories, Mama Sadhbh.

AMALA *shoots* MAMA CAROLINA.

Bang Bang Bang.

AMALA *shoots* SADHBH.

Bang Bang Bang.

AMALA *runs and takes aim at the audience.*

Bang.
Bang.
Bang.

The End.

Ariel Dorfman
DEATH AND THE MAIDEN
PURGATORIO
READER
THE RESISTANCE TRILOGY
WIDOWS

David Edgar
ALBERT SPEER
ARTHUR & GEORGE *after* Barnes
CONTINENTAL DIVIDE
EDGAR: SHORTS
THE MASTER BUILDER *after* Ibsen
PENTECOST
THE PRISONER'S DILEMMA
THE SHAPE OF THE TABLE
TESTING THE ECHO
A TIME TO KEEP *with* Stephanie Dale

Helen Edmundson
ANNA KARENINA *after* Tolstoy
THE CLEARING
CORAM BOY *after* Gavin
GONE TO EARTH *after* Webb
LIFE IS A DREAM *after* Calderón
THE MILL ON THE FLOSS *after* Eliot
MOTHER TERESA IS DEAD
ORESTES *after* Euripides
WAR AND PEACE *after* Tolstoy

Samantha Ellis
CLING TO ME LIKE IVY

Stella Feehily
DREAMS OF VIOLENCE
DUCK
O GO MY MAN

Debbie Tucker Green
BORN BAD
DIRTY BUTTERFLY
RANDOM
STONING MARY
TRADE & GENERATIONS
TRUTH AND RECONCILIATION

Sam Holcroft
COCKROACH
DANCING BEARS
PINK
WHILE YOU LIE

Lucy Kirkwood
BEAUTY AND THE BEAST *with* Katie Mitchell
BLOODY WIMMIN
HEDDA *after* Ibsen
IT FELT EMPTY WHEN THE HEART WENT AT FIRST BUT
IT IS ALRIGHT NOW
TINDERBOX

Liz Lochhead
BLOOD AND ICE
DRACULA *after* Bram Stoker
EDUCATING AGNES ('The School for Wives') *after* Molière
GOOD THINGS
MARY QUEEN OF SCOTS GOT HER HEAD CHOPPED OFF
MEDEA *after* Euripides
MISERYGUTS & TARTUFFE *after* Molière
PERFECT DAYS
THEBANS

Conor McPherson
DUBLIN CAROL
McPHERSON PLAYS: ONE
McPHERSON PLAYS: TWO
PORT AUTHORITY
THE SEAFARER
SHINING CITY
THE VEIL
THE WEIR

Chloë Moss
CHRISTMAS IS MILES AWAY
FATAL LIGHT
HOW LOVE IS SPELT
THE WAY HOME
THIS WIDE NIGHT

Rona Munro
THE HOUSE OF BERNARDA ALBA
after Federico Garcìa Lorca
THE INDIAN BOY
IRON
THE LAST WITCH
LITTLE EAGLES
LONG TIME DEAD
THE MAIDEN STONE
MARY BARTON *after* Elizabeth Gaskell
PANDAS
STRAWBERRIES IN JANUARY
from Evelyne de la Chenelière
YOUR TURN TO CLEAN THE STAIR & FUGUE

Bruce Norris
CLYBOURNE PARK
THE PAIN AND THE ITCH

Nina Raine
RABBIT
TRIBES

Lou Ramsden
BREED
HUNDREDS AND THOUSANDS

Diane Samuels
3 SISTERS ON HOPE STREET *with* Tracy-Ann Oberman
KINDERTRANSPORT
THE TRUE LIFE FICTION OF MATA HARI

Ali Taylor
COTTON WOOL
OVERSPILL

Jack Thorne
2ND MAY 1997
BUNNY
STACY & FANNY AND FAGGOT
WHEN YOU CURE ME

Enda Walsh
BEDBOUND & MISTERMAN
DELIRIUM
DISCO PIGS & SUCKING DUBLIN
ENDA WALSH PLAYS: ONE
THE NEW ELECTRIC BALLROOM
THE SMALL THINGS
THE WALWORTH FARCE

Nicholas Wright
CRESSIDA
HIS DARK MATERIALS *after* Pullman
MRS KLEIN
RATTIGAN'S NIJINSKY
THE REPORTER
THÉRÈSE RAQUIN *after* Zola
VINCENT IN BRIXTON
WRIGHT: FIVE PLAYS

Steve Waters
THE CONTINGENCY PLAN
FAST LABOUR
LITTLE PLATOONS
THE UNTHINKABLE
WORLD MUSIC

A Nick Hern Book

Bang Bang Bang first published in Great Britain as a paperback original in 2011 by Nick Hern Books Limited, 14 Larden Road, London W3 7ST, in association with Out of Joint and the Royal Court Theatre, London

Bang Bang Bang copyright © 2011 Stella Feehily

Stella Feehily has asserted her right to be identified as the author of this work

Cover image © Gabriel Moreno
Cover design: Ned Hoste, 2H

Typeset by Nick Hern Books, London
Printed and bound in Great Britain by CPI Group (UK) Ltd, Croydon, CR0 4YY

A CIP catalogue record for this book is available from the British Library

ISBN   978 1 84842 211 7

CAUTION   All rights whatsoever in this play are strictly reserved. Requests to reproduce the text in whole or in part should be addressed to the publisher.

Amateur Performing Rights   Applications for performance, including readings and excerpts, by amateurs in the English language throughout the world should be addressed to the Performing Rights Manager, Nick Hern Books, 14 Larden Road, London W3 7ST, *tel* +44 (0)20 8749 4953, *e-mail* info@nickhernbooks.demon.co.uk, except as follows:

Australia: Dominie Drama, 8 Cross Street, Brookvale 2100, *fax* (2) 9938 8695, *e-mail* drama@dominie.com.au

New Zealand: Play Bureau, PO Box 420, New Plymouth, *fax* (6) 753 2150, *e-mail* play.bureau.nz@xtra.co.nz

South Africa: DALRO (pty) Ltd, PO Box 31627, 2017 Braamfontein, *tel* (11) 712 8000, *fax* (11) 403 9094, *e-mail* theatricals@dalro.co.za

USA and Canada: Casarotto Ramsay and Associates Ltd, see details below

Professional Performing Rights   Applications for performance by professionals in any medium and in any language throughout the world (including by stock companies in the USA and Canada) should be addressed to Casarotto Ramsay and Associates Ltd, Waverley House, 7-12 Noel Street, London W1F 8GQ, *fax* +44 (0)20 7287 9128, *e-mail* agents@casarotto.co.uk

No performance of any kind may be given unless a licence has been obtained. Applications should be made before rehearsals begin. Publication of this play does not necessarily indicate its availability for amateur performance.